Knock on the sky and listen to the sound.

Zen Saying

The Secret Lives of Chickens

or Tales from the Chickenyard and Beyond

by Sunny Franson

ISBN: 978-0-9855109-7-8
Reformatted, Second Printing, August 2015
Art and Nature

Printed and Distributed by Ingram Content Group and Lightning Source
Ingram Content Group
14 Ingram Boulevard
P.O. Box 3006
LaVergne, TN 37086

First Printing September 2012
ISBN: 978-0-9855109-0-9
Printed in the United States of America
RJ Communications
New York, NY 10017
(800) 621 2556

Dedicated to Sarge, who was one special rooster.

Contents

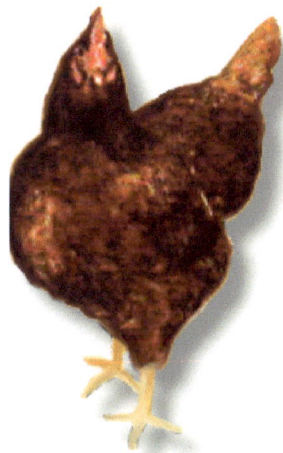

Acknowledgments

The first acknowledgment is offered with heartfelt thanks to all the chickens that were such inspiring little beings. They are the best. The second goes to the myriad furred, haired, scaled and other individuals that interacted with chickens, even those who ate them, because that's nature, even when it's devastating because some fine feathered friend vanished from your life one day.

Many thanks to Bob and to all my family who always offered advice and supportive thoughts. Many relatives, friends and neighbors cheered on my efforts to write about chickens. I can never thank them enough for the faith and good will that they offered, so I thank them all collectively. A few reviewed earlier copies: my cousins Don and Marilyn Graham and Johanne Franson, and dear friends Carl and Linda Alford, Stan and Char Choate, Cecil and Carol Prack and Justine Smith. Meyo Marrufo helped with a cover design for a cd. Friends and neighbors Chuck and Sharon Coburn and family, Jim and Mary McKinney and family and Ed and Frances Seely and family know the area quite well, and some knew many of the individual chickens too. Pete Stillman allowed me to photograph his friendly and lovely Silky hen. Ines and Walter supported the unsure individual that I was while working on this book.

Others who showed an interest in the book and who therefore helped me to persevere are Susan Huppert at Homegrown Press, the folks at SelfPublishing and Create Spaces, Elaine Belanger at Backyard Poultry magazine, Roni McFadden at The Biscuit Press, the folks at Lake County Arts Council and Gualala Arts Council, the various folks who are involved with the local writers' circle and writer's workshops, and many more. When someone taps you on the shoulder and says, "Hey, that sounds great", or "Hey, that sounds like fun", it's a lift that needs to be acknowledged. Maybe they weren't even sure of the effect they were having, but I was, and I'm grateful.

The vast majority of the images are of the first chickens, their lives, and then, of those that came after. A very old Brownie Instamatic was the camera. It was essentially a box, but I was very fond of it, and it was sturdy and reliable. Unfortunately one day, as it sat on a counter, it came apart. All four sides fell away from the top and bottom, all at once, all out flat. More recent images were digital, but the little Instamatic left its legacy.

Introduction

When I was small, my grandfather who lived with us at the time enjoyed his chickens and the chickenhouse that he and my dad built. It was a very nice house, worthy of any chickens alive in those days. It kept them warm in winter and cool in summer. I didn't realize what a nice chickenhouse it was until later, when it was transformed into a small barn for my horse and survived the transition very well, because it had been built to be quite large and strong. I loved my horse. I didn't really remember the chickens.

Meanwhile, my older brother who was in 4H raised chickens for his project and showed them at the county fair. His red rooster, General Oswald, won a blue ribbon and then lived out his life in our back yard. There were lots of flowers in the flower beds and there was quite an expanse of lawn, and the yard was fenced and safe for General Oswald, keeping neighborhood animals out although the General could have flown away if he'd wanted. He chose to live there with Bunny No Good, a very large white rabbit that had outgrown his hutch. The only dog that watched them was our wonderful dog Mopsey. She never touched them, although she would lie down near them and watch their every move, her mouth watering.

Many years and many life experiences passed before I was around chickens again. These were "my" chickens, but that doesn't fit, because chickens don't seem to belong to anybody but themselves and aren't really in your life. Either they live alongside you, or you are in their lives. They have enchanted and fascinated me ever since.

They have helped strengthen for me the notion that all life on our planet has more innate intelligence than our species has ever allowed itself to believe, imagine, or even speculate might be the case. After you live around chickens and observe them over a period of time, you begin to understand that those little feathered beings that are generally considered to be creatures that lay eggs and that are the subjects of infinite recipes, and not much more, do have complex lives after all. They exhibit behavior that follows social rules and that reveals intricate relationships. Because they cluck, shriek, whistle, coo, and chuckle for instance, and we don't, does not mean that we can assume that there isn't much happening behind those bright, beady eyes or beating within those small, strong hearts.

Chapter 1

Sarge

Sarge and His Hens
Their First Home
Discoveries

He arrived one cold, winter day with four fat red hens that he watched and herded. He clucked to them and he fussed over them. They were his.

Sarge and His Hens

He was a shiny brown and black oblong of hormones, stalking regally along on two scaly legs with two gigantic feet looking vaguely like clawed tripods. He had a tapering neck, a smaller head, maybe an even smaller brain, and two round, beady eyes that were a luminous red-orange. He also had glistening blue-black tail feathers that curved upward in an elegant arch, and then cascaded gracefully back and down, so that they rippled and shone in the sun as he walked.

On the top of his head there was an amazing scarlet comb that more or less gave him the appearance of wearing something outlandishly decorative. He had impressive wattles too, huge and bright red, swinging freely back and forth under his chin with every step he took. He also had a very large bill that could hurt you if he wanted to use it, but he was not aggressive toward people.

He had a pleasant nature, but at the same time he was protective of his small flock, and he took his duties very seriously. Although he constantly watched over his hens, we were ignored and were gently guided toward the inevitable understanding that these chickens were a group unto themselves, and that people usually didn't matter to them, because people weren't members of their flock. Over time we came to understand that chickens can and do relate to other species, but they still have very specific and strict social rules and are oriented toward their own kind. Chickens don't appreciate being separated from other chickens, and chickens without other chickens seem to be very lonely and run with anxious delight toward another chicken when they see one.

The hens that arrived with the rooster were smaller, bottom-heavy versions with shorter tails, slender legs, smaller wattles and combs, but only slightly smaller feet. While he strode about crowing, clucking, whistling, and shrieking, the hens cooed and chuckled softly to each other like contented red-brown powder puffs, while they scratched for insects, worms, and any other food that they could find. They were always looking for food.

Their First Home

Their first chickenhouse was in the back corner of a large, very old barn, but not long after that, we constructed a better home for them on the east side of the barn, where they could enjoy the morning sun. Meanwhile they lived in the back corner because along one side of the barn wall was a small opening, and if you were a chicken you could make your way through it to the great outdoors beyond. For your convenience there was a long ramp to the ground outside. There was also a small door that was hinged to the barn wall at the opening, and after all the chickens had trooped inside for the night, this door was closed to keep out skunks and raccoons. They love chickens, and a sleeping chicken is nearly comatose and an easy target.

It was dark back in that corner, but we tried to make them all feel at home, with mounds of fresh pine shavings everywhere in their home and spread deeply in three roomy nest boxes along the back wall. We noticed that even though there were three nest boxes, the hens used only one nest box, and they generally argued over it when they wanted to lay their eggs. They also liked the nest boxes for roosting rather than the roost we provided for them, and as dusk fell into night, all five huddled together on the top of about one and a half nest boxes. When they fell asleep, they looked like a single snoring bundle that gently rose and fell with each breath. This seemed to be a waste of space because they could have spread out very comfortably, but as time went on, we came to accept that chickens are unusual beings with alien ways.

After a few months, the truly magnificent rooster became known as Sarge. Because of his behavior there was really no other name for him. The hens had to follow him everywhere, and they couldn't lag or he would complain and shove them along. He was the leader, the rooster-about-town, and he was in charge of them all. If he wanted the group to search for bugs up the dry creek bed, they would march along in single file behind him until he stopped. Then they would begin to scratch and forage, all five of them.

The old barn was located maybe a few hundred feet behind the house, and the house was located about the same distance from the road. The barn was a little to the west, and what you saw looking back from the west side of the house was the barn's front door. Large, mature walnut trees at the edge of an aging orchard grew along the barn's west and north sides, and a creek ran along its east side. The creek came from hills to the north behind the barn, where it ran through pear and walnut orchards on its way to a seasonal lake. When the creek reached the barn, it created a cool and inviting area for the chickens.

A large garage between the house and the barn partially blocked the view of the barn from the house, important when you wanted to know where the chickens were, and when the chickens didn't want you to know where they were. The front of the barn faced civilization, but its back faced the winding creek, orchard, hills, predators and food. The chickens lived on the edge.

Discoveries

Because I knew next to nothing about chickens, what I learned through the years was by observation and by having them as friends, and eventually by having one of them as an enemy. Simply by existing, they taught me everything I learned about chickens.

They had a blank page to fill any way that they wanted, and I think they knew this from the very beginning. They had me completely under their spell, and they were well aware of it.

We may have been friends, the chickens and I, but we were friends on their

The old barn had a lot of character.

terms, as if I were friendly with fluffy pterodactyls. They didn't adapt to me. I adapted to them and learned to arrange my life to do what was necessary for their lives.

Probably the first lesson I learned about chickens was that they had their own ways and you had to work with those ways, because you would never get them to change. If you wanted something that they didn't want, you had to outsmart them and basically let the chips fall where they might. Contrary to popular opinion this can take some doing, and it might not work anyway.

Whoever began the rumor that chickens are not very bright must have assumed that because they are domestic birds, they are basically how people think that they should be. But chickens are shrewd and cunning, and they have minds of their own. They have some different goals than we do, that's all.

Their primary, immediate, and all-consuming concern is food, and there are complex social regimens associated with finding, claiming, and eating food. As far as a chicken is concerned, its bill and those huge feet are all that it needs. Edging some cracked corn away from a hen eating it can be risky, and they use those bills well.

Chickens are individuals just as we are individuals and some might behave more aggressively than others, but all of them spend their days finding, keeping and eating food.

It was peaceful behind the old barn.

There were rumors that roosters might attack you, especially when your back was turned, so just after the small group arrived, I found myself nervously swiveling about to check on Sarge's whereabouts when I was around the chickens. I didn't need to do this, because Sarge really didn't care about me at all.

He liked that food was always available in the feeder, and he would puff up, fuss, and call the hens to eat every morning when their feeder was filled and they were given fresh water. He came to anticipate this golden opportunity for showing himself as the best provider ever, watching the feeder intently and uttering small shrieks as soon as it was full, and I moved a few steps away from it. He coexisted amiably with us, with the cat, and with the dogs, not backing down from anyone but not provoking anyone either. We really didn't rank in his world, since we weren't hens, danger, or food.

It was easy to fall under the spell of softly clucking hens and a haughty rooster. It was pleasant to understand that their daily lives were really very detailed and required far more awareness from them than anybody thought they possessed. They were utterly charming.

Sarge was protective of his small group and constantly guarded and patrolled the perimeters of his kingdom. This meant looking up, looking down, and looking all around three hundred and sixty degrees, since for a chicken, danger could be everywhere.

Often, danger arrived in the form of a neighbor's unpleasant dog that seemed to enjoy killing, never eating what it killed. When Sarge's group was small, this dog never caught a chicken. However when the group grew larger a few years later and it was more difficult to see where all of your hens were, four hens died at the jaws of this dog, whose otherwise affable owner excused everything it did.

When Sarge saw danger coming from far across the orchard, he would holler and shriek. He was so loud that he could be heard across fields a quarter of a mile away. His alarms came in different values and sounds but the danger alarm was piercing, it always carried over all parts of the orchard where the hens were at that moment, and Sarge always knew where they were.

If Sarge shrieked because the sneaky dog happened to be around, the hens and Sarge would be up the ramp and inside their house literally in a flash. This disagreeable dog couldn't manage the door to their house because it was too small, much to the dog's frustration, and the chickens were safe at least for the moment.

The chickens only emerged from a safe place when they were absolutely certain that danger had passed. It was hard to tell exactly how they knew when it was safe to head back outside to scratch for food, loll in the sun, or relax in the grass, but they always seemed to know. I figure that the senses of chickens are truly vastly underrated.

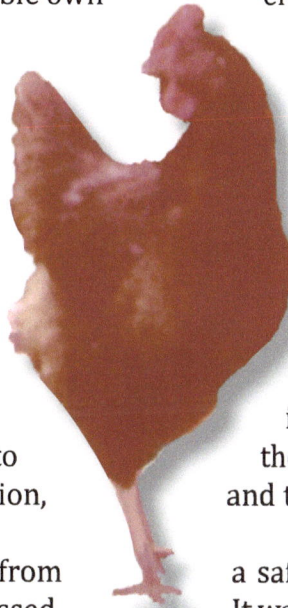

Chapter 2

A Day with the Chickens

At Sunrise
At Noon
At Dusk
Chickens in Spring, Summer,
Fall, and Winter

Chickens are cyclical creatures, predictably awake and eventually cheerful at sunrise, and groggy and sluggish at dusk. You have to admire them for being the feathered stoics that they are, following the rules day in and day out, even though you know that nature intended them to be that way. Nature intended inclinations for all of us, but it seems that sometimes some of us don't religiously follow the rules like chickens do. Chickens don't seem to know much about pretension.

At Sunrise

By and large Sarge and hens enjoyed a daily routine that started by waking at daybreak with the hens chuckling gently to themselves and Sarge crowing his heart out. It never seemed that he was greeting the day as people say roosters do. It was more like he was re-establishing his presence after a night of silence. After all, he crowed now and then throughout the day, usually when a hen laid an egg and clucked afterward, or when he found a particularly nice mass of grubs or worms for the hens, and they happily gobbled up everything. Or when he noticed a hawk circling or perching on a nearby limb, and sounded an alarm that brought everyone inside until the hawk had gone and it was safe to come back outside. Or basically when anything happened that seemed to leave him in the enviable position of being the smartest, most special rooster in existence.

Maybe crowing was his way of telling the world that he was wonderful, even though his crowing seemed to happen more at some times than at other times. But he really was wonderful, and apparently it was important for everyone to know that the flock was safe and would prevail, and that his hens would carry forth his genes into posterity.

In the early gray light the hens chortled softly among themselves, beginning to stir with eyes still bleary from sleep, still breathing deeply, moving a little here and stretching a little there. They slept so soundly at night that unless they were disturbed, they didn't immediately awaken but took some time to bring themselves to a conscious state. As the light grew they moved about a little more, eventually stumbled away from their roost, and began to look around for breakfast. If for some reason you happened to be in the chickenhouse unusually early and they saw you as something unfamiliar, they would be startled and become rapidly alert, but generally they were like someone who needs a few cups of hot coffee.

Once they made their way down from their roost to the floor, which was the main room and had soft shavings, a raised feeder, and water dish, they began pecking at their first food of the day. The door was generally opened early for them, and some of the more confident individuals made their way outside, standing in the growing light and looking around. Orientation didn't take very long, and within minutes they began to look for food.

Foraging was a prolonged activity in the morning, but when the sun was up and the chickens were feeling content, having assuaged immediate hunger, they enjoyed taking time to simply stand in the sunlight and soak it in. As soon as the morning dew was gone, they took breaks from scratching and hunting for food and lolled on grassy areas in sunshine, languidly stretching out wings and toes in the warmth.

Generally by midmorning, they began to lay eggs, and this continued on through early afternoon. Now and then there would be an egg in a nest very early in the morning or even well into mid afternoon, but most of the hens preferred late mornings for laying their eggs. Each hen had her own precise, timed, egg-laying cycle, and although cycles were similar for all the hens, they were not exactly the same. Laying eggs usually happened over a few hours' time for the main group of hens, and that meant each one's need for a nest box overlapped others' needs. Thus, pecking orders were reinforced.

The chickens spent their mornings in this pleasant and relaxed manner. If left to their own devices, with no pressures from a hawk, the neighbor's miserable dog, or other outside intrusions, they foraged and rested in comfort, wandered and foraged, and laid eggs and foraged all morning long. In summer they were more active in the early mornings, but as days grew shorter they found themselves out and about a tiny bit later each day. They followed the sun.

At Noon

When they first arrived, they took only a day or so to settle into a routine that was pleasing for them, up in the morning, eating, relaxing, heading outside, scratching around, relaxing, eating some more, wandering in search of food, fluffing and relaxing, still eating, all day long. During the heat of the noonday sun, they liked to loll in a depression of some soft dirt where they had created a dust bath, or if it was too hot, they liked to settle down in a shady area under a shrub or a tree.

In the late morning and early afternoon, there were continual side trips for laying eggs. The hens were very good about using a nest box for this. One by one, they made their way with care and determination back to the chickenhouse to a nest box. They rarely laid eggs on the ground or in a clump of grass.

Actually they normally argued over who got to be in the nest box first, and also over who could stay the longest. This wasn't as obvious when the flock was small, although the pattern was still there. They all seemed to want to use the same nest box, and the privilege of getting it seemed to revolve around a pecking order. They generally ignored the other nest boxes. Around late morning the targeted nest box was a crowded area, with hens hanging over the edge or maneuvering their way inside, sometimes settling in sideways or crunched up against the hen that happened to be in it already.

Meanwhile, clucking took on a different tone. The "rrrrrrr" sounds they made weren't soft and cooing any more but were low, sort of rumbling, and even threatening if you were another hen. They actually pecked at the hen in the box or at the hen that was in their way, although no one was ever really hurt. The Nest Box was a staging area.

You chose your nest.

You checked for rivals.

Once she laid her egg, a hen climbed out of the nest box generally without a sound but then right away hollered "cut-cut-ca*daw*kit" over and over again. Meanwhile the next hen in line instantly snatched her place. The business of laying eggs provided a window into a society in

You claimed the nest.

which a pecking order was vital and important, where it was constantly re-established, and where it was continually reinforced. Strict rules were an integral part of this business, just as they were a part of chicken society in general.

As the flock grew larger over time, more nest boxes were added and more were used, but the hens never used all of the nest boxes, choosing a select few instead and arguing over them. Now and then they changed their few favorite nest boxes around, leaving previous favorites alone. Why they did this was a mystery.

Maybe it was chance, but you never thought about chance where chickens were concerned because in spite of their endearing manners, they had firm and complex rules in their lives. You didn't always know what the rules were, because you weren't a chicken and they didn't share with you. You were basically ignored, but it was easy to see that rules existed.

During the time that the chickens lived out of that small corner in the back of the barn, there were fields of oats and vetch in the orchard around two sides of the barn. In the spring these fields grew thick and tall, so tall that if a hen were hunting bits of food inside them, she couldn't be seen. There were insects in there. Some areas stayed moist longer than open ground, and this meant worms. The small flock loved to work its way through those fields.

The only way of knowing where they were was from the sounds they made, like Sarge's shrieks and the hens' cooing and chuckling. If Sarge were to stand up very straight, you could just make out the comb on the top of his head. It looked like a very ripe, elongated, slender, and serrated tomato moving along just above the thickest growth, weaving its way through thinner stands of waving stalks that reached above the more lush patches and that supported seed heads dripping with oats. The hens were lost from view because they were too short.

Directly across the road from the house, in part of a small orchard, lived a very nice, elderly lady who had chickens of her own, a variety called Black Minorcas. These hens were a friendly, gentle, talkative group. The lady didn't have a rooster but did have a few dozen of these hens, slightly smaller than Rhode Island Reds but with the same pear shapes. The Minorcas were very striking with black, shiny feathers and contrasting bright red combs. They were free-ranging hens and often wandered to the edge of her property, close to the road lined with large, old oaks with grasses beneath them, excellent scratching grounds for bugs.

When these hens were close to the road, their red combs and black, shiny bodies were easily seen from the west side of the barn. In early spring, if you were Sarge or one of his hens, you would have difficulty seeing the Minorcas because your view was deep within the oats and vetch fields. However, your hearing could pick up the placid, contented sounds they made as they foraged.

One fine spring day, Sarge and the hens were scratching about, just behind the barn, making their way around it into a part of the orchard directly across from the Black Minorcas' home. Sarge and the hens were several hundred feet from the road, a safe distance for a group of comfortable, settled chickens intent on finding bugs and worms, relaxing during the midday heat, taking an occasional sip of water, and in general hanging out.

In spring, oats and vetch grew into a lush, delicious outdoor restaurant, if you were a chicken.

Suddenly a red comb shot up just above the oats and vetch. It was visible at an angle, not quite broadside to us from our vantage point, so its owner was looking in the direction of the road. It was a large, magnificent comb, very long and fire-engine red. The comb perked up, became absolutely still, and then as though it had been shot from an arrow, raced along the tops of waving oats and green vetch, heading toward the road. It moved fast, completely apart from the ground, a disembodied, speeding red comb.

When it reached the road, the rest of Sarge appeared as he bolted across and launched himself toward the black hens which immediately scattered, because they hadn't seen what was coming at them at full speed until he was already there. He shrieked and clucked loudly, trying to round up his prizes, and was distraught when I arrived to herd him back to his house. The Minorcas didn't welcome him at all. They were too busy running in the other direction, toward the safety of their own home.

He went back across the road, slowing traffic and regally ignoring confounded expressions and angry hoots from motorists, but he made it. He joined his own flock and never again tried to reach the Black Minorcas. Their behavior must have been a scorching blow to his pride.

At Dusk

As the day faded, so did the chickens. Toward the day's end, they seemed to be in a special space and time when they were in limbo between enthusiastically scratching and eating all day long, and when their internal twenty-four hour clocks were winding down toward slumber. They seemed to have a last burst of energy just before the waning daylight began to slip away and dusk emerged, when that change from day to night seems to accelerate.

During this last burst of energy, you saw Sarge marching up the dry creek bed in summertime, hens clipping along behind him in single file. Or at any time of year you saw Sarge wandering out into the orchard, hens close by but fanning out in all directions, all scratching vigorously and looking intently for food.

Then as if by magic, everyone began to move in slow motion. Almost in unison the chickens turned around and gradually made their way back to the chickenhouse. This took a while because their pace became slower and slower. They scratched and ate as they went, moving with an almost lemming-like quality as they drifted inexorably toward their house. At first, right after that last burst of energy and food, they seemed alert and comfortable, but the closer they moved to the chickenhouse, the more dreamlike their movements became. They floated along. They weren't like robots but were more like fluffed manifestations of a kindly honored tradition that won't ever change. It was like the difference between being brainlessly directed and being happily content with the given universe. They cooed very softly to themselves.

By the time they arrived at the door to the chickenhouse, they moved even more slowly as they traipsed up the ramp and made their way into their house, with food and water, and fresh shavings on the floor. They wandered over toward their roosts and nest boxes, hopped up onto the ledge where these were, and began to settle themselves onto a few favorite nest boxes for the night. By this time their necks had slackened a bit and their heads were bowed. Their eyes weren't very bright, and their eyelids had become very heavy.

If you startled them for some reason, they'd look alert with those beady bright eyes carefully watching you, but only for a very short moment, and then lids would droop again. If you quietly watched them and didn't startle them, they would fall fairly quickly into a stupor. The soft murmuring faded, and finally everyone was quiet, bundled together, breathing more and more deeply until the feathered mass gently rose and fell, rose and fell. The chickens were asleep for another night. The door at the top of the ramp leading into their house was latched, and they were safe until morning.

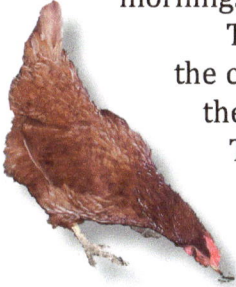

There were always a few stragglers that didn't quite arrive back at the chickenhouse along with the main group. Sarge was generally with the main group and by this time was just as quiet as the hens were. The stragglers were usually only a few moments behind, and as the group settled in for the night, it was always the entire group.

At first we wondered if these stragglers were outcasts or were the lowest of the low on the pecking order, but they seemed to be able to settle in with the main group with no problem at all. Nobody shoved them around. Now and then we saw a few hens settling themselves in tandem with everybody else, but we understood that at the root of it all, the integrity of the flock was of the utmost importance, and that included the safety of all its members. As time went on, it seemed that the latecomers might be outcasts to some degree but more to the point, they were the free spirits of the flock. They were the hens that were outside first and inside last, they ranged a little farther afield than anybody else, and they seemed to create more consternation in Sarge than the others did. At least they appeared to be the ones he frequently herded back to the main group, shrieking all the way.

One winter day as dusk was approaching, the chickens were milling around, snatching a morsel here and there, and slowly beginning to follow that urge to wander toward the chickenhouse and settle in for the night. This particular day was one in a series of very rainy days, and the creek was full with water running swiftly only a few inches from the top of its banks.

To be able to visualize the true dilemma of the chicken that swam, it helps to know a little about the creek. It was basically a runoff creek, although for most of its ancient history it had been the major channel for water from a very large watershed and had run the year around. Nearly a century before, when the main channel had been re-routed so the rich soil in its basin could be cultivated, this part of the creek had become smaller over time, although its watershed was still extensive and a huge amount of water surged through it during winter rains. It was known to overflow its banks on occasion. It ranged from perhaps five to seven feet deep and was maybe ten to fifteen feet across, and when it was full its current was extremely swift. No one would have wanted to be caught in that current, and we were always very respectful of it during high water.

If a hen were on the garden side of the creek scratching contentedly in the moist, fragrant, garden soil, and she wanted to make her way back to the chickenhouse but was directly across the creek from it, the best way when the creek was full was to track downstream along the creek, away from the chickenhouse for maybe sixty or seventy feet, cross the footbridge that was there, and then walk back up the other side of the creek to the chickenhouse. This was the way the chickens returned home for the night when they had been foraging in the garden that was fallow in winter, and when the creek was running.

They all knew how to do this and there weren't any problems, except on this one particular day. There was a hen that generally ranged a little farther away than the others and tended to come in just a few moments later than the others. She was something of a thorn in Sarge's side. On this day she didn't wander on down to the footbridge with everybody else but kept scratching and eating in the garden, while the others slowly and quietly made their way down to the footbridge, carefully across it and up the other side of the creek, and then one by one up the ramp into their house. Most of the group was still outside but close to their house, when the lone hen suddenly realized that she had been left behind and was all by herself on the wrong side of the creek.

If you were a chicken, you looked from the garden to the footbridge when water was high and you wanted to go home. You left the garden, crossed the footbridge, turned right and made your way upstream on the other side of the creek.

Now chickens are a communal lot and don't like to be away from one another. They're insecure about that and will dodge you and run away so they can stay close to everybody else. When she noticed that she was alone, this hen became frantic. She was so upset that she forgot about the footbridge and ran for short distances back and forth along the creek, calling out to the others that were directly across from her. It was really too bad that a muddy torrent of swiftly moving water maybe ten or twelve feet across was between her and the others.

She grew more and more frantic, calling "Cccrrreeaaaaaawww....," long, mournful sounds which seemed torn straight from her heart. She took the tension as long as she could, and then with a giant leap, she took off flapping, feet still running in mid air, and landed in the middle of the creek. It was a sad, sad moment. I was also on the garden side of the creek and thought it was all over for her, but no, there she was, or at least there was her comb and outstretched bill right in the middle of the creek, being carried away by the current. The comb and beak were jerking along and you could imagine the huge feet, unwebbed, thrashing for dear life underwater. I ran alongside the creek, hoping to somehow grab her before she disappeared, although I had no idea how to do that.

Then a miracle happened, and the red comb in the muddy water was moving closer to the opposite shore, although still moving downstream. On the other side of the creek, just above the footbridge, a strange, frightening creature hauled itself out of the creek, wobbled a little, and began to slowly weave back and forth as it made its way back to the chickenhouse. It didn't look like a chicken. It didn't even look completely alive. It was a dark, sodden mass stumbling toward the chickenhouse door.

I got there in time to carefully pick her up, examine her, and towel her off, but what she wanted most was to curl up in the bundle of hens settling in for the night. She was warm and still had dry skin of all things, but I thought she might become chilled anyway.

The anxious and mournful cries she expressed when I tried to remove her so I could keep her warm and dry and observe her through the night, were not only heart-wrenching but were also so unnerving that

After crossing the footbridge, you traipsed back upstream to your home.

I allowed her to stay. She screamed pitifully, and it worked because she stopped as soon as I released her. It was almost dark, but finally there she was, in the center of a mass of fluffy, warm hens, looking exhausted but basically all right. The next morning she was fine, but her ordeal seemed to have left her in a sober frame of mind, and thereafter she was unwilling to stray very far from the main flock, even though she was the chicken that could swim.

Chickens in Spring, Summer, Fall, and Winter

The chickens' behavior seemed to be strongly influenced by cycles of many kinds. On a day-to-day basis their twenty-four hour clocks reigned supreme, but they also responded to seasonal changes and annual cycles too. Theirs was a multi-layered approach to life.

Winter gradually gave way to the crisp, bright days of early springtime. The chickens grew ever more active as days became longer, fresh grass grew, flowers began to appear, and there were more insects in the air and on the ground. The world began to wake up.

So did the chickens. It was the time for new life and more eggs. Each hen, at least each young or middle-aged hen, began to lay nearly one egg per day. Spring means renewal, and more eggs would have meant more chicks if eggs hadn't been collected every day.

For some reason these particular hens didn't attempt to create their own special nests in which to incubate eggs or even to show signs of wanting to set on eggs. Apparently many planned generations of their kind had resulted in a reduction of the brooding instinct. Now and then one would briefly consider setting on eggs, but that was unusual and short-lived. The usual cycle of setting on eggs in late spring, raising chicks in summer, and seeing them into adulthood by late fall and winter didn't seem to appeal to these Rhode Island Reds. The idea of reproducing the flock from itself was appealing because these were really very sweet chickens, so a few years later, long after they had been in their new, larger home, we decided to introduce a few Silky chickens to the flock.

Silkies are small chickens with beautifully soft feathers that look like haloes of white light surrounding their bodies. Their extremely fine feathers fluff out like Christmas angel hair and seem just about as delicate, but are actually strong. Silkies often have bluish combs,

You watched after your fellow chickens. You were a flock.

30

tongues, feet and skin. There are Silkies of many colors, but Silkies with white feathers are quite simply walking powder puffs. Silkies are renowned for their gentle natures and for their mothering instincts. Who could miss with kindly natured and beautiful Silkies that would also raise Rhode Island Red chicks?

There were only a few Silkies at first, although more came later. They were a treat to have in the flock, they stayed to themselves, and they incubated and hatched Rhode Island Red chicks. They were ideal mothers that wouldn't allow the babies out of their sight, making certain each soft, tiny chick was kept safe and warm within white, downy feathers. Because of the fine and fluffy nature of Silky feathers, it was often difficult to see where wings actually were when they were folded next to the hen's body. Little yellow heads popped up from where you thought soft white wings were folded over them. The Silky mother watched you with a beady black eye, she hunched down in her nest as you came closer to her, and if your hand strayed too close to her brood because you wanted to hold those soft, little chicks, she nailed it with her sharp bill. Those bills were hard.

The plan worked. Chicks became a part of the annual chicken cycle. Chicks grew into chickens, and hens that passed away from natural causes were replaced. Natural causes were basically the only causes for a hen's demise. Part of the idea had been that we would supplement our food supply with the extra roosters, but that didn't work. They were too individual, and we'd known them since they were chicks. Luckily there happened to be an outlet for them at a nearby pet store. It would have been nice to keep all of them, but excess roosters would have argued heatedly with each other, and this little flock was a peaceful group with Sarge remaining in control.

The days lengthened, temperatures rose, and summer eventually arrived. Before the longer days became too hot, and during breaks in their foraging and scratching, the chickens loved to take time during the day to loll in the warm sunshine. The first time I saw them do this I was alarmed because they were stretched out on their sides and looked as though they might be drawing their last breaths, but they were only taking in the relaxing sunshine and absorbing it. They even stretched out those long toes, flexed their wings, and looked completely at ease, like someone luxuriating in a wonderful spa. They didn't make much noise and had sleepy, heavily lidded eyes. Eventually they got to their feet, stretched each wing including wing feathers, stretched out legs and toes, briefly shook and ruffled themselves, and began to scratch and eat again.

As the days grew warmer, they began to spend their breaks under a shady plant, shrub or tree, and in the hottest part of the summer, they found shade where the ground still retained some moisture. They scratched the ground until little chicken-sized depressions were everywhere, then fluffed themselves, and settled into a cool place for a nice break from the hot sun.

This caused some problems because they always found the places that had been most recently watered. Usually this was somewhere in the flower garden or lawn, where the moist earth produced lovely roses, annual flowers, and nice patches of cool, refreshing grass. If you didn't catch the chickens right away and send them back in the direction of their own house, you'd find numerous depressions and half scratched up flowers and lawn that you had lovingly planted and cultivated, meanwhile watching buds form and anticipating their opening into delicate flowers. The chickens in a flower bed of annuals were like bulls in a china shop, except that rage or fear wasn't the driving force. Finding insects and worms was. Bits of torn petals and tender leaves were strewn over scratched out beds of soft earth that you'd carefully nurtured and mulched, now transformed into little mounds and chicken-sized depressions.

This cat and mouse game continued all summer long. It became intense as the soil continued to dry under the summer sun, as temperatures rose, and as irrigated areas were ever more the only soft, moist places around. It was very difficult to keep the chickens out. They were like the tide. You couldn't stop them.

Only when days began to noticeably shorten, when temperatures began to cool, and especially when a late summer rainstorm softened the soil and you inhaled that wonderful smell of freshly moistened earth, did the chickens begin to stay out of the flower beds around the house and lawns. Fall was just around the corner. During the heat of summer the hens didn't lay quite as many eggs, and now they stopped laying and began their annual molt.

Every year toward fall the chickens began to lose their old, sometimes scruffy feathers in preparation for fresh new ones. A year of dust baths, summer sun, rainstorms, fluffing, wandering, foraging, and sleeping had taken a toll, and older feathers were sometimes ragged and twisted. These chickens had a nice home to protect their feathers, but they still needed new ones each year. Molting was serious. It wasn't just about losing feathers and growing new ones. Other metabolic changes went along with losing feathers. One's comb grew pale and appeared smaller, and one had bare patches with short, stubby, new feathers here and there on one's body. In general one's overall appearance was bizarre.

They must have known this because their behavior changed too. Molting chickens seemed to retreat and make themselves smaller. Those hens normally at the head of the pecking order seemed to fade into the background during their molt.

Sometimes it was even difficult to recognize them because characteristics they had, like Crooked Comb's crooked comb for instance, changed while they were molting. Crooked Comb had a tiny, ridged, pinkish comb when she molted, but the bright red one that fell to one side like a rakish hat from the flapper era reappeared after she had grown fresh, new plumage. You could still recognize her during her molt, but for its duration she remained in the background, only reclaiming her place of second or third in the pecking order after her new feathers were grown and her comb and behavior had returned to normal. The behavioral change during molting made sense because one was after all a whole chicken, infinitely more than a sum of chicken parts. Although a hen didn't lay eggs when she molted, the hens didn't molt at exactly the same time, and there were still fresh eggs now and then.

The chickens and their new feathers were ready by the time shorter and colder days arrived. They didn't appear to be chilled when they were molting even though they didn't have many feathers, and there were patches of dark pink, bare skin at times. This was another mystery associated with chicken physiology.

During winter months the chickens liked to be outside whenever they could, although rain discouraged them and sent them running back to the shelter of their house or to the nearest dry place. Snow was infrequent, a good thing because they didn't care for it and stepped gingerly into it with toes outstretched, clucking under their breaths. On nippy days when the sun was out, they were clever about finding a warm, dry spot, generally near a building, preferably where sunshine bounced off of any reflective surface and onto their feathered bodies as they stretched out to catch the sun's rays. Bundling together at night was important for warmth, but they always bundled together anyway even during the heat of summer months, because they were a social lot.

They always looked like they were enjoying life regardless of what season it was. They slumbered on during longer nights but were active and happy during daylight hours. When spring began to roll around again, they began to lay more eggs. Like all of nature, the chickens' own seasonal cycles continued on and on, endlessly, over and over again. Like all creatures without pretense, the chickens were happily in tune with the earth.

Chapter 3

The New House

Sunshine
The Creek
The Fence

The barn where the chickens lived was large and old, built around the turn of the twentieth century, and had several walled-in sections plus a second floor with solid stairs running along one side up to the second story. You had to approach the stairs from just inside the back of the barn, and you climbed them easily because they were wide and deep although there was no railing. When you reached the top floor, you experienced the size of the whole barn on one huge second floor. There were large openings along the sides and the front of the second floor, and one especially large opening was fitted for what was probably a place for a winch or pulley at one time.

For some reason, the chickens never wandered up to the second floor, but we all did. It was wonderful up there and provided places for birds to stay out of the rain and to roost on cold winter nights. The evidence was always there.

The barn had been used for many purposes during its lifetime, most recently for drying walnuts. Downstairs it had low, very slightly slanted, four or five foot wide drying shelves that ran nearly all the way across the width of the barn. The shelves lined both sides of two walls which divided the first floor into three fairly equal sections, front to back. These walls had very large and widely framed open doorways, all in a line along the west wall of the barn. You could walk the length of the barn with ease, and you could see the back when you entered at the front.

The drying shelves in the middle section stretched up to the barn's east or creek side, where there were generous, window-like openings cut into the outside wall and conveniently lined with chicken wire.

After some months of living in the shadowy depths of the back corner of the barn, the chickens moved into a new home built for them where these windows were located, so they could enjoy the morning sun. The flock was also expanding, and they needed a larger place.

We walled off an area on the east side of the middle section of the barn, building a chicken wire wall, framing and creating an area of maybe twenty-five feet long between the two inner walls, and maybe ten or twelve feet across. The chicken wire was cut to surround the shelves and was stapled onto them, the framing, the walls, the floor, and the ceiling, creating a completely enclosed new chickenhouse. We framed a door into the middle of the chicken wire wall, so we could enter the new chickenhouse from within the barn. Inside the new chickenhouse we set nest boxes on those slanted shelves, lining them up along the back walls, and shimming and leveling them.

At floor level in the barn's outer wall, between the two large window openings in the new chickenhouse, we sawed open a chicken exit to the outside world. The sawed-out square of wood was fitted with small wooden crosspieces and became a hinged door for the small opening. The door could be latched shut, keeping the chickens safe at night when predators might otherwise find a fat feathered meal ready for the taking. A small ramp led to the ground outside.

Sunshine

This particular area worked out perfectly for the chickens' new home. After a night of slumber on their chosen nest boxes, the chickens awakened to the eastern horizon, sunlight slanting directly onto them through the windows. They stretched toes and wing feathers while making their way across fresh pine shavings to the edge of the shelf. They hopped down onto a bench conveniently placed at the base of the shelf, and then on down to the floor into more fresh pine shavings, where they found themselves at their feeder and waterer.

Morning sunlight beaming in the windows of the new chickenhouse was just the ticket. The chickens sought out these beams, soaking them in before breakfast. Then the door to the outside was opened and sunlight streamed in, beckoning the chickens toward the great outdoors. Another new day began and the chickens were always happy about that, even though they weren't completely awake yet.

Their new ramp to the outside world wasn't as large as the one they'd had before, and it didn't have small cross pieces of wood like the first ramp did. It didn't need to be large or fancy, because it didn't stretch very far. The barn was leaning, and its flooring was closer to the ground on this side than it was on the other side. However at that time the barn was still very solid and rarely squeaked when you walked through it. It sat quietly like a sturdy wooden toad on a patch of level ground, reaching out toward the creek water nearby.

Many years later, the barn began to lean more precariously at an alarming rate which increased daily, long, square nails popping out at you as you walked by, and

If you were a chicken and had sneaked into the garden, you saw the barn through the marigolds of summer. Home was the area protected by visqueen that kept out wind and winter chill.

eventually it needed to be taken down board by board. That caused an exodus of rats that had been living undetected in its depths. Groups of rats left from the back of the barn every evening just before dusk, so after supper some family members and friends relaxed out behind the barn with twenty-twos, visiting, and dispatching rats. For a month or so this was an evening event, but by then the chickens had been long gone from the barn and were in another new home.

Meanwhile the chickens lived very comfortably for several years in the new area on the east side of the barn. This location was well suited to them with its sunlight, large windows, large ledges for nest boxes and for roosts, easy access to the land and creek outside, and maybe best of all, directly across the creek from the rich garden soil and several grapevines that produced tasty seedless grapes every year. It was ideal.

The Creek

As the chickens made their way outside every morning, they looked like a fairly solid rust colored mass slowly making its way down the chicken ramp. They could walk about ten feet toward the garden before they reached the creek, dry in summer but with running water in late fall, winter and spring. Since the creek ran parallel to the length of the barn and about ten feet away from it, maybe the creek was the reason that the barn's foundation had become much shorter on this side, causing the barn to lean toward the creek.

This small creek was central to the chickens' lives, so a better picture of it deserves some attention. It had smooth banks since it was kept gently graded and open, because it was a runoff creek and needed to function well. Otherwise barn, garage and house could have been in trouble during heavy rains. It was dry in summer and fall, sometimes frighteningly full in winter, and generally had running water at least from late fall until the early summer months began.

Before it reached the barn, it formed a few graceful bends as it wound its way through orchards and past a large blackberry patch. In the spring its banks were grassy and full of wildflowers. When it was running, gently rippling mosses and water plants grew in fine silt residue in its bed. It became a rich, watery environment in the spring and was home to lots of insects, worms, tadpoles and frogs, and even a species of fish endemic to the area. They used it to migrate to marshy fields near the hills, where they spawned in flooded, shallow, grassy meadows.

The creek attracted an enormous variety of birds from songbirds to ducks, reptiles like lizards and snakes, small mammals like squirrels, raccoons and opossums, and a few larger ones like mountain lions, bobcats and bears. For a few years there were bear tracks on its banks, and there were always many other kinds of tracks too. It also attracted chickens.

When they had discovered this creek shortly after they arrived, the chickens were ecstatic, clucking, cooing, whistling and shrieking.

If you were a chicken and you looked in and around this creek, bugs were flying around your head at your level and were crawling away from you at your feet, you saw tender plants to eat, and there was soft earth for you to scratch. Chickens like to scratch. What they really do is fiercely dig and kick backward, soil flying in all directions. In fact sometimes you can't see a chicken, but you can see dirt flying and mounding up around what you know must be a chicken. A soft, moist area where they can scratch for bugs is heaven and draws all chickens.

They all loved the creek. It was a sumptuous smorgasbord to which they returned over and over again, especially during that time in the spring when its banks were very green and running water only covered several inches of creek bed. All that damp earth around the creek and along its banks was ready made for breakfast, lunch and dinner. Generally they ate in the morning, relaxed in the sun for a while, and then headed up the creek in the afternoon, finally turning around and eating their way back to the chickenhouse. Sometimes they made a last dash up the creek for food before retiring for the night.

If you were standing just behind the barn with your fellow chickens, just past the culvert, you saw a banquet unfold before your very eyes.

Sarge usually led them when they were purposefully making their way up the creek, and normally they all stalked along in single file. If you were standing a distance away from the creek, generally you couldn't see any chickens, because they were somewhere on its banks and were too short to be seen. But you could often see a large red comb making its way upstream. You'd hear whistles and calls and you'd know that the chickens were on the move. Until we became more familiar with their habits, we worried about them while they were in the creek, because it was also a path for nighttime chicken predators whose fresh tracks were visible in the mud, but the chickens were always out of the creek before sunset.

In late spring, when water was low and they were able to simply wade across the creek, the creek was still their own personal restaurant, and not much was growing in the garden just yet. In summer, the creek bed grew dry and hard and was no longer inviting to the chickens. Instead, they headed toward the soft earth and delicious plants now growing in the vegetable garden, easy to do because there was no water in the creek, and with a few quick steps they reached their target. Gardens are ambrosia for chickens, and when they lived directly across from the vegetable garden, it was fenced with removable netting while vegetables were growing. That was the only way. Otherwise there would have been no garden at all.

As the year progressed and the creek dried, and it became less inviting as a source of food, it was still crisscrossed by the chickens as they made their way here and there, out into the orchard or toward the garden, or further downstream toward flower gardens and lawn, searching for food and snacking on bugs along the way. Depending upon the time of year, the creek was a place to eat, a place to cross, and a place that provided an easy route to and from the chickenhouse.

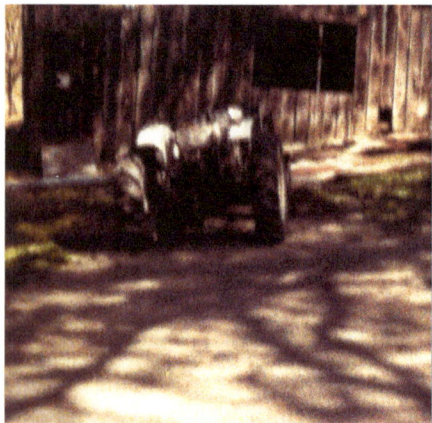

The tractor was usually parked conveniently close to the chickenyard, well within earshot of alert chickens.

Any time the tractor was out grading the creek, the chickens were in seventh heaven and fanned out behind it, delighting in a whole new supply of bugs and worms exposed in the freshly turned earth. As soon as the tractor started up in the morning, there were the chickens, running to position themselves behind it as fast as their legs could carry their round, feathered little bodies. They called out to each other, rolling from side to side as they hurried to follow the tractor up and down the creek.

Since the tractor also tilled the orchard, it became a doubly important piece of equipment to the chickens. One tilling happened in fall, after harvest and before the orchard was seeded with oats and vetch that helped to enrich the soil, at just about the same time when the creek was graded, usually not long before water began to run in it again. Much to the chickens' delight, another tilling happened in early summer when the tractor was out in the orchard, cultivating the crop of vetch into the soil.

The cover of healthy vetch, growing tall in the early summer sun, provided ample cover for small life of all kinds, and when it was plowed under, the unwary lost their lives to sharp-eyed chickens. The chickens were omnivorous and even chased

40

mice that lost their homes to the cultivator and tried to run away. Years later there came a time when our thoughtful, kind neighbors looked after the chickens at their house, as we moved into a house nearby and built the chickens yet another home. These neighbors were astonished when they discovered that within the flock were some very determined mousers. It was clearly a case of opportunity knocking because the chickens didn't scout for mice, but when one ran across their floor, they pounced.

Meanwhile, in the orchard the chickens followed the tractor in a formation not unlike the "V" formation in which geese fly. The tractor was the leader at the head of the "V", with the chickens spread out in a single row on either side. Up and down, row after row, they followed the tractor that was cultivating as it went. It was not moving quickly and was almost in sync with chickens on the hunt.

Rich, crumbly soil mixed with tilled vetch remained moist for a long time after cultivating was over, and earthworms were everywhere. The chickens were in chicken heaven. When you watched the chickens over several days' time, it was clear that they didn't simply react to the tractor and its work. They observed it carefully and optimized every opportunity that it offered, remaining alert to every move that might mean that the tractor would be out and about.

In winter when the orchard was muddy, when water began to run in the creek again and it was perhaps half full, the chickens crossed the creek by using either the footbridge to the south of their house or a narrow road over a small culvert in the creek, just to the north of their house. However the culvert periodically washed out, and then the only way for them to cross the creek was the footbridge. This old wooden bridge was slightly lower than the tops of the banks of the creek were. The result was that when water was very high, the footbridge was under a few inches of water. It was heavy and was well anchored, so it didn't float down the creek, although there were rumors that it had escaped in years past.

The culvert disappeared in high water, and the foot-bridge was the only way back to the chickenhouse.

If you crossed the footbridge when it was under water, you felt as though you were unbalanced even though you weren't, because there was moving water all around you. You clung to the handrail for dear life.

It must have been a strange sensation for the chickens to cross the footbridge when creek water was just level with the top of the bridge, but they crossed the bridge anyway and never seemed to be caught as water crept up over the top of the flooring of the bridge. Somehow, they knew when this was about to happen and invariably crossed just before they might have to wade.

Once in a great while, one or two were just a little late in crossing the bridge, not a wise decision. If runoff were increasing, not lessening, and they found themselves on the vegetable garden side of the creek, they'd have to wade right in.

They generally seemed to be very alert to this possibility and were caught off guard only once or twice, and only when water was just barely covering the footbridge. They hated that and lifted each giant foot high, one after the other, delicately shaking each foot as they stepped,

When the creek was full with runoff from the hills and valleys of its fairly large watershed, the footbridge was in danger of going under water. Water swirling around your feet was not comforting. It would have been even worse for a small, helpless chicken.

and made their way somewhat gingerly across the footbridge, complaining all the way.

They were definitely more aware of rising water than the rest of us were. We finally learned to watch them and came to depend on their instincts about this.

The Fence

After the chickens had lived in the sunlight on the east side of the barn for a while, a design for a fence for both chicken and garden security was made. The fence would restrict the chickens to the land that was along the entire east side of the barn. The resulting chickenyard would be narrow since the creek was close by, but it would be probably sixty or more feet long. There would be plenty of room within the chickenyard. In any case a door was planned at one end, and that door would be open nearly all of the time, allowing the chickens to range in the orchard and creek as usual.

Tall posts went in, corners were strengthened with diagonal posts, and a tall door frame was constructed. Rolls of chicken wire were placed in position and began to be stretched out along the fence framework and nailed in place.

A door was completed, framing for it was hammered into place in the fencing closest to the garage and house, hinges were secured on the door and the framework, and a strong hook and eye latch to keep the door closed was securely fastened into position.

As the fence went up, the chickens watched carefully. It was clear that they realized that something important was happening and that it would affect them. They were actually obviously dismayed only after the posts were in and chicken wire was being stretched along the posts.

On that day, it was dusk and most of the chickens were already inside their house. Our timing was deliberate because we didn't want stragglers to be fenced out. After all, the chickens needed time to adjust and to become acquainted with the layout of their new chickenyard and the location of its door.

As the last bit of wire went up, three hens in the chickenhouse came to their small door, moved slowly down the ramp, looked around, and stood at the base of the ramp. One faced north, one faced east, and the third faced south. The ramp, chickenhouse and barn were directly behind them to the west. They stood there, each looking outward in the direction she was facing. Each hen remained stock still. Heads were raised, eyes to the front, and then in unison, heads were lifted back and bills opened. All together in a chorus, they uttered soft, low cries. Their cries were plaintive and even sounded mournful. They continued to cry out for several minutes, heads up and back, standing straight and still, round bodies backed up to the ramp, each looking straight ahead to the north, east, and south.

They knew what had happened. That couldn't have been more obvious. What they didn't know yet was that they would be ranging almost as much as before but would be secure inside their yard when no one was at home to protect them, when the neighbor's unpleasant dog was about, when too many predators' fresh tracks were around, or at some other time when they were not very safe. Or when no one was around and the garden was not safe.

In fact, in time they grew accustomed to running at top speed, giant feet in the way and round bodies rolling back and forth, into their chickenyard whenever danger seemed close by for one reason or another. Sarge was especially pleased to be able to call them into the chickenyard when he sensed danger. He assumed the role of benevolent protector, as though he had built the fence and created a safe haven for them all by himself.

Along the creek side of the new fence stood a large, mature walnut tree. This tree was only a few feet from the culvert that occasionally washed out during winter rains, near the northern edge of the chickenyard. Its branches were well above the new fence and draped over the chickenyard toward the barn, providing a shady area for the chickens during summer months. This was important should the chickens find themselves incarcerated in their chickenyard, unable to find moist, shady places in the yard or the garden.

The tree was also a beautiful addition to the landscape, graceful limbs nearly reaching the old barn and many well above it, leaning over the creek, and shading a pool created where water emerged from the culvert downstream, when the creek was not running full. In hot summer months chickens were sheltered by the shade of the tree. In fall, golden leaves and mature walnuts fell into the dry creek bed. In winter, this tree held the soil as swirling water rushed through the culvert and over the tiny roadway when the creek was very full.

The creek was an interesting place, up close or far away, in the day and at dusk.

In spring, fresh green grass grew along the edges of the pool beneath the tree just as new leaves were beginning to grace its limbs. Spawning fish circled and rested in the pool before facing the modest current in the culvert as they headed upstream, water skeeters darted across its surface, other insects swam in it, and dragonflies and

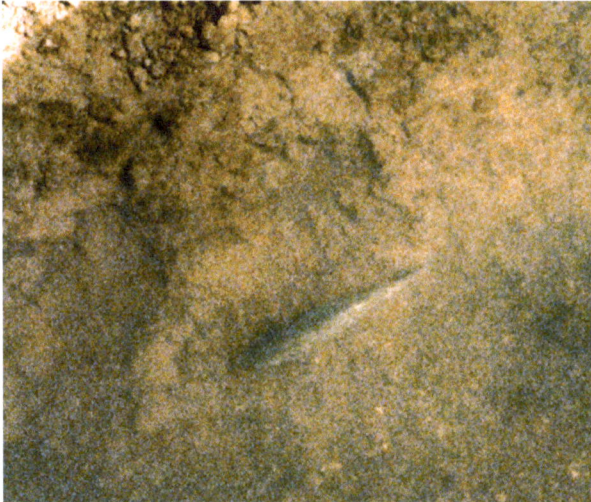

damselflies flew over it. Numerous tracks of many sizes and shapes appeared along its banks and all along the creek for that matter. Chickens chuckled softly to themselves as they wandered along its edges under the tree, and as they settled themselves comfortably in the shade.

This tree created a small ecosystem at one end of the chickenyard, both within the fenced chickenyard and outside of the fence. Inside the chickenyard it made a nice, shady niche in which the chickens

Local endemic fish migrated up feeder streams and spawned in shallow areas. They came, spawned in the fields above, and left in the blink of an eye. We never saw them or their hatchlings leave.

could safely relax. Just outside the chickenyard, it offered shade and soil protection in areas under its limbs, and rich habitat within its branches for many creatures including birds. Not far from its base and in its shade, the creek bank was mossy, and algae and water plants grew prolifically in the little pool.

Naturally wildlife was attracted to this lovely microecosystem. Birds flew into the tree and perched on its branches, eyeing the little pool and the insects hovering above it. Near dusk an owl could be heard hooting close by, not surprising since small mammal tracks were easily visible near the water's edge. Then a red tailed hawk began to perch on a sturdy branch just above the chickens and their chickenyard.

Initially the hawk seemed to require no further thought because Rhode Island Red chickens are not small, and these chickens were portly to say the least. They were at least as large as the hawk. Perhaps this particular hawk was young and inexperienced, because one day there was a flurry of activity on the ground just outside the chickenyard, probably twenty feet to the south of the tree trunk. It looked like a flapping bunch of wings going in all directions. There were more colors in there than rusty red, and then the hawk emerged. It was on the ground and had backed away from its prey that happened to be Crooked Comb.

Crooked Comb was not a retiring chicken, being at least third place but usually about second place in the pecking order, and once in a while even in first place. She screamed and she fought. She didn't run away. She attacked the hawk that was lying half on its side by this time, wings outstretched.

Of course Sarge heard the commotion and shrieking as he ran, he hurried into the fray. He also attacked the hawk, beating his wings at it and going after it with his bill and the spurs on his legs. Everyone else was standing around exclaiming and watching with avid interest.

Finally the hawk managed to escape the furious chickens, and it flew up into the tree. I watched it stay there for a few moments before it made the very unintelligent move of trying to grab Crooked Comb once more. The battle started again, wings flapping wildly, with mostly hawk feathers flying. After a much shorter time the hawk flew up into the tree again, remained there for a brief moment, and then flew away. It didn't return.

Meanwhile, within minutes Crooked Comb became her outwardly serene self again, and Sarge eventually calmed down. No one wanted to see a beautiful and courageous creature like a hawk injured, so a life-sized plastic owl, a replica of this hawk's natural predator, was swiftly purchased and was anchored in the tree in a manner that we hoped would appear natural. No hawk ever again perched in that tree to observe the chickens.

It had been fascinating to watch this drama unfold. If there had previously been any doubt that the flock was multitalented, purposeful, and autonomous, the last remnants of doubt were gone. More than ever we realized that we were merely guests in the chickens' personal world and that the flock was one with nature and with its environment, probably more so than we were in ours.

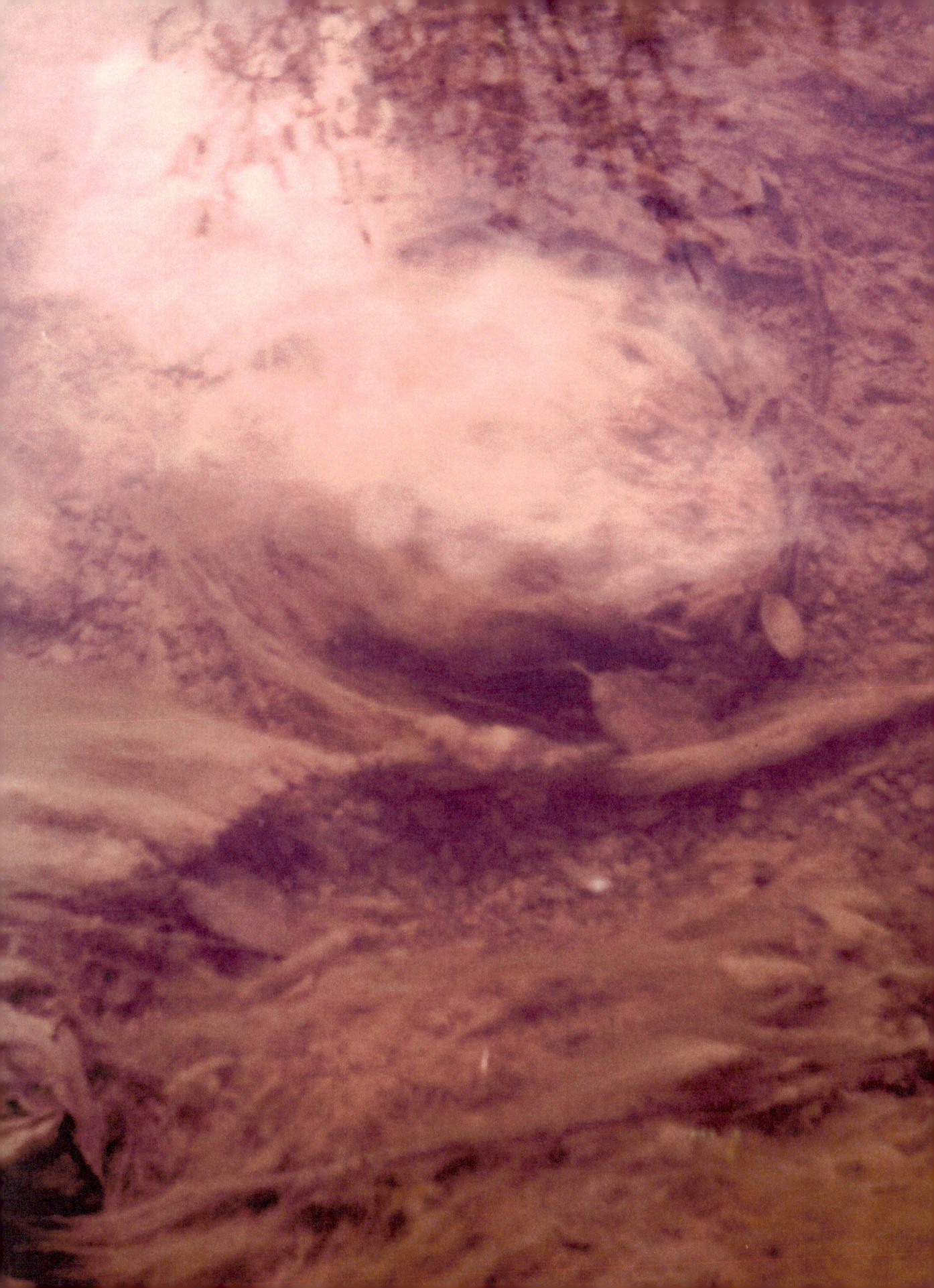

Chapter 4

Chickens and Food

Chickens and Bugs
Chickens and the Puppy Food
Chickens and the Vegetable Garden
Chickens and the Flower Gardens
Chickens on the Back Stoop

If you knew anything at all about chickens, you knew that the term "food" was ever-present with any part of any thought about living, breathing chickens. This did not mean food for anyone else, like unpleasant dog, raccoons, and skunks, or fried for humans, but rather about chickens living, breathing and forever foraging. It was a universal constant.

Chickens and Bugs

It's only fair to mention that despite being essentially something of a despot, Sarge searched for food for the hens. He was especially good at finding bugs, including large beetles. He pushed these around with his bill so they couldn't get away and called out to the hens with a "Crrpp, crrrpp, crrpp," a loud, staccato sound that the hens knew well, because they came running and flying as fast as their fat feathered bodies would allow them to move. They looked like rusty red metal shavings do when they're very close to a large magnet. The lucky hen that was the first to arrive would get the bug. If Sarge found a group of bugs or a soft, moist spot with several worms, the faster hens grabbed the prizes. They looked like the shavings that are closest to the magnet.

Sarge didn't eat when he called his hens to food he'd found. He always saved the food for the first hen to arrive. When everyone was happily scratching and finding food here and there, Sarge also scratched around and ate. However, as soon as a particularly juicy but unwary bug tried crawling from under one rock to get to another one, Sarge was generally on it in a flash, comb slashing through the air, calling out "Crrpp, crrpp, crrpp," the lunch bell. Hens came running, wings flapping to help speed them along.

If the bug were a large bug, the first hen that grabbed it ran away with it, around a corner if there was one close by, and dodged everyone else who chased after her, bills stretched out to grab it away from her. The hen with the bug didn't always manage to evade the others, and sometimes a second hen succeeded in getting a firm grasp on the bug, running off with it or with some of its parts. Then everyone chased that hen. Some hens were very good at eating on the run because if you stopped to eat, you could lose your prize.

Sarge watched this drama with rapt attention, uttering small whistles, cries and low clucks, the hens whipping past him, back and forth. Once the morsel was gone, the group settled down to some serious scratching until something else was spotted and the drama happened all over again. Sarge didn't tolerate any excessive force except his own and didn't allow hens to be very aggressive with one another. He maintained a sort of stable chaos, like a benevolent tyrant.

The only food in the form of something that crawled, that we saw the chickens avoid, were very large slugs. They would have been easy targets since they couldn't move quickly, and they were plentiful in moist areas under shrubbery, on the ground near shady sides of the barn, or anywhere that water collected. Perfect places were along irrigated grassy areas next to a building. Not only were slugs comfortably resting there, but also chickens were happily settling into these cool areas on a hot day. One would think that slugs would be an ideal food source for the chickens but for some reason, perhaps size, flavor, texture or something else, they left slugs alone. It was a little unnerving to observe chickens avoiding large slugs as a food source because there wasn't much that they did avoid. The discrepancy was glaring.

Chickens and the Puppy Food

As a rule a few of the hens would take the initiative to range out and about searching for food, although Sarge often struck out as their leader, stalking up the creek for instance. Although he held onto food for them when he spotted it, the hens themselves were usually more aggressive about checking out new areas when foraging afield. Finding food was a very serious business.

That's how they found the puppy food.

A puppy came into our lives and into our hearts. He stayed with us, but his food supply stayed in the garage, where one or both garage doors were open during the day. Dry puppy food has considerable protein in it, and apparently chickens can

smell protein for miles, it seemed.

The first time that we knew they'd found the puppy food, they'd managed to overturn the bag and had dumped it everywhere, eating themselves nearly sick and then finding a nearby tree and lounging in the shade. After that, we watched for them whenever we were around the puppy food. When they came back for more, we chased them away and figured that they had learned that they couldn't invade the puppy's food supply. We were so incredibly naïve.

They waited until they thought that no one was around, and then they made their move. However we were inside the garage, and we watched. They didn't walk noisily around the corner and through the open garage door, like chickens looking for food would normally do. Instead, they used stealth. We heard nothing, but for some reason we looked up from what we were doing at the time, and there, near the ground at one of the garage door openings, was something red. It moved away, then it came back, and then a yellow bill and a beady eye appeared around the corner of the open garage door. Ever so slowly a neck and then a rust colored, feathered body came around the corner, the hen moving quietly and slowly, looking around to see if the coast was clear.

One by one, in single file they came, heading straight to the puppy food. Not a cluck was heard.

Somewhere in the middle of the group was Sarge, as quiet as everyone else. Until they hit the puppy food, that is. At first they ate for a few moments. Then their joy at finding this food overwhelmed them, they couldn't contain themselves any longer, and they all started to exclaim at once, especially Sarge who behaved as though all by himself he had discovered the mother lode. The more they ate, the more they clucked and called to whoever wasn't there yet. They were in that happy state of the oblivion of a feeding frenzy, like chocolate lovers who

Bo came first.

51

Loki came later.

unexpectedly come upon a free, luscious mound of creamy milk chocolate dotted with pieces of fresh, moist marzipan. It was ecstasy in motion.

Eventually the puppy food was moved to a chicken-free location but not before everyone was enchanted and stupefied by the chickens' stealthy behavior. It was astonishing that chickens could plan their moves with such quiet precision.

Chickens and the Vegetable Garden

The bag of puppy food may have been like the butter on daily bread for the chickens, but the vegetable garden was like the organic honey dripping from the bread and butter. The garden soil was already good soil and had been enriched with mulch and with natural fertilizers. It was home to large earthworms and many bugs, per square foot. During the growing season, there were plants that had tasty leaves, and there were moist, tilled areas with tender seedlings that were supposed to develop into lettuce, cabbage, broccoli, or other vegetables.

It was shocking to see how much earth and how many seedlings could fly in all directions with only one swift scratch of a huge chicken foot. When the chickens were scratching they used both feet, one after the other, scratching the earth back behind them and then eating whatever was fresh and tender, crawling away, or running for its life after its home had been destroyed. The chickens routinely scratched all day long regardless of the season, especially enjoying scratching their way up the moist creek bottom in late spring before it was quite time for the garden. They knew every year when to stay in the creek bottom, and they knew when to hit the garden with its delicate, moist seed beds and tender early crops.

It became abundantly clear that the garden needed a protective barrier, and bird netting normally used for crop protection worked very well. We stretched it around poles, keeping it about five feet high. Smaller, leaner chickens might have chosen to fly over this barrier and into the garden, but for the plump Rhode Island Reds, five feet was high enough. The netting was doubled so it was quite visible to smaller birds, and it was crumpled at the bottom.

Finding an opening at the bottom was difficult, although the chickens spent many long hours looking for one. If they tried to scratch at it or maneuver it around, they ran the risk of becoming entangled in it. Then they had to cry out until they were freed, or until they loosened it enough for their escape. This only happened a couple of times over a period of many years. No one was ever hurt since the netting was soft and pliable, and the chickens quickly learned how to avoid becoming entangled. Smaller birds were never caught in it, but years later one snake was.

The chickens generally couldn't find a way to get through the netting, even though they continued to try. Over time and in the summer sun, as it weakened and tore here and there, they managed to find any vulnerable place and make their way into the inner sanctum. The garden probably appeared like a leafy gourmet banquet to them.

They were quiet as they made their way into the garden proper, just as they had been quiet at first when scouting out the puppy food. Unless you were actually in the garden at the same time that they found a way into it, and you saw them, it wasn't easy to know that they were there, until you saw destroyed vegetables and stalks strewn over the ground and holes dug around established plants that were wilting.

Many of the vegetables that were growing provided ample cover for them. Unless you were within hearing distance, you might not know that they were scratching and tearing tender shoots apart. They could be out of sight on the garden's far side, behind the corn patch for instance, between rows of corn taller than they were, or among

During summer, when the chickens gazed across the creek as they were emerging from their open gate, they took in breakfast, lunch and dinner in the grapes and garden beyond.

bushy green bean plants. It was a fairly large garden. It was like an old-fashioned malt shop.

The chickens especially liked vine-ripened tomatoes. They browsed around the tomato plants, hidden from sight by the leafy growth, pecking here and there into the juicy, red, tomato flesh. That they didn't eat a whole tomato but just pecked at tomatoes at random while they wandered around, leaving ripe tomatoes with holes in them, was especially frustrating for those of us who loved fresh garden tomatoes. Any tomato with a few pecks in it was vulnerable and would spoil almost within hours unless it was found, picked immediately, cleaned well and then used, providing there was enough left to use after you had generously cut away the damaged areas. You could only make so much tomato sauce.

Fresh greens and soft dirt - who could resist?

When the chickens were full they lounged and rested in the moist, cool earth in the holes they had dug. They chuckled softly among themselves. When you heard those sounds coming from somewhere in the garden, you knew there was trouble and that for some hapless vegetables and maybe for part of your dinner, it was already too late. You knew that you had to get the chickens out of the garden, find where they had breached the walls, make repairs, fetch a hoe and rake, and rebuild the garden as best you could.

If you'd been waiting for an especially large tomato to fully ripen before you picked it, or for a few more leaves to grow on a particularly succulent head of leaf lettuce before you brought it in, and you found those pecked, torn and strewn over the ground, you might have become emotional when surveying the wreckage. There is no easy fix for a vegetable that has been ravaged by chickens.

You just had to remember that the chickens were after all much smaller and apparently more helpless than you were, and that according to almost all conversations and clichés about them, also much less intelligent. However the truth of all of this had become serious food for thought and was increasingly more difficult to accept. It appeared that those clichés were only about what you were supposed to believe and not about what you constantly observed.

Chickens and the Flower Gardens

Flower gardens edged the lawns, and the chickens gravitated toward both the lawns and flower gardens during the hot summer months. Lawns and flower gardens surrounded the entire house, patio, and front porch, meaning there was considerable habitat for the chickens to invade, to explore, to enjoy, to scratch, and to destroy.

The flower gardens along with the lawns offered variety from the usual territory claimed by the chickens, and variety was the spice of life. There were corners

You saw even more of the vegetable garden when you were closer to the footbridge and the back yard. You saw the garden's moist, freshly cultivated soil, perfect for scratching out bugs and worms. You noticed the melon plants running down the dry creekbed, and you knew that your nostrils would let you know when the delicate melons were ripening and ready for you to peck. All you had to do was to wait and plan your attack.

behind which to hide and observe, wide stretches of cool lawn on which to settle when enjoying a break from foraging, cool moisture from watered lawns to enjoy on a hot day, and close by, soft, moist earth to scratch, where flowers were carefully tended and encouraged to grow and bloom.

If you lounged in a flower bed, why not enjoy one with delicate, beautiful flowers carefully nurtured from seed or young plants, offering a soft cushion upon which you could fluff your feathers? You could also lift your head and grab at a passing beetle or jab at an earthworm moving just under the soil's surface.

The flower bed closest to the chickenhouse was a large circular area at the edge of the back lawn. A path led alongside it to the footbridge that crossed the creek to get to the garden. This area was behind the house and near the garage, and it reached to the creek. Part of it bordered the creek bank, and it was a remnant of a lovely shaded glen that had existed there when a huge bay laurel and an enormous wild grape vine had still been intact.

A century or two earlier the grape vine had attached itself along one side of the bay laurel, and through the long years of their lives together, had actually pulled the tree into a slanted position, carrying them both out over the creek, toward the orchard on the other side. Vines were anywhere from six to eight inches in diameter and covered an area perhaps thirty feet across and perhaps eighty feet from the ground to the top of the tree.

The bay laurel's trunk itself was around five to six feet in diameter. On the creek side of the garage and extending from the tree trunk to the creek bank, the huge wild grape vines had created a semicircle that was secluded and cool.

It was a beautiful, gentle habitat that invited wildlife during the evening and the night. I saw a deer and her fawn sleeping there during one summer. I also saw raccoons climbing through the tree and vines, sometimes accompanied by our large orange cat that seemed to be at home with most visitors.

The bay laurel together with the wild grape vine leaned out over the creek and footbridge.

The old tree and vine had formed a lovely glen.

However this very large cat would also jump onto the backs of invading dogs. He was fearless when he felt the need to protect his territory.

One winter an unusual and heavy snowstorm overloaded the leaning trunk and branches of the bay laurel. With a resounding crash, its trunk broke and fell out over the creek, which thankfully wasn't running yet. The tree was already bearing the weight of the enormous grape vine, and the extra weight of the snow was too much for it. Fortunately no one was beneath it when it fell. We managed to clear away debris and create a better path in the creek, a good thing since within a few hours about two feet of melted snow water was running in it.

The remaining tree was perhaps forty or fifty feet tall and had branches that grew out from the trunk beneath the place where it had broken. It was still a good-sized tree but was not the behemoth that it had been, and the shady glen was gone. In its place, after the huge mound of tree branches and wild grape vines was cleared, was the open circular area that became a home for sun-loving jasmine, miniature roses, a strawberry bed and an herb garden. Naturally the soil that had been part of a woodsy habitat for at least a century and that was now frequently watered, was rich and moist, home to a multitude of tiny life, and it was a chicken comfort zone on warm

When viewed from the garden, the fallen tree and vine were still half as high as the house.

spring days. This circular area was also the first line of defense against the chickens.

They found it quickly enough. It was after all close to the footbridge that they used to cross the creek in winter when the creek was flowing. It wasn't as inviting during the winter months as the garden area that they loved and targeted, but as spring passed into summer and days grew warmer, the garden was fenced off and this moist, circular area was an open invitation for them to scratch out little chicken hollows and loll in the warm sun, after destroying miniature rosebuds, new basil and new rosemary tips.

It was difficult to keep them out during the brief time when this area was still moist and inviting, when strawberries were ripening but before the intense summer sun had arrived. It was an area that was still watered during summer, but after the great crash of tree and vine, it was in full, hot sun. During the heat of summer, it became more of a path through which the chickens slowly and inexorably moved on their way to flower gardens and lawns, in shadier areas further away from the chickenhouse.

Lawns were inviting especially when moles made fresh mounds of earth in them. A patch of fresh dirt on a lawn was ready-made for scratching for bugs and worms. You could never find enough scratched out, scattered soil to rake and fill the depressions that the chickens made, a maddening dilemma and difficult to understand, since all of the available soil had come from exactly that mole mound where now there was the depression you were trying to fill.

Violets bloomed over much of the back lawn in spring. Beyond lay lush stretches of oats and vetch with occasional wild mustard.

The back lawn, a lawn that came to within a few feet of the house, bordered the circular herb garden and strawberry bed. It also bordered a bed of roses with daphne, azaleas and camellias that were next to the creek. The creek continued south toward the road, separating the orchard from flower beds, lawns and house.

Flower beds ran the length of this part of the creek, a buffer between the creek and the front and back lawns, and the patio at the side of the house. At the edge of the front lawn, daffodil beds continued by the side of the creek all the way to the road. At that point the creek left the property and ran under a bridge. Since there were flower beds creekside, they were vulnerable to the chickens that could either move across lawns to reach them or, conveniently hidden from view, could make their way down the

creek bed during the dry seasons.

On the other side of the house was the driveway to the garage and barn. It was bordered by more flower beds and then more front lawn. A sidewalk went from the house down the middle of the two front lawns to a circular driveway, off of the main driveway. Beyond the front lawns, the semicircle within this circular driveway was filled with yet more lawn and was encircled by yet more flower beds. A large bird bath surrounded by daylily beds was at the center of the semicircle.

There were perennials, annuals, shrubs of all sizes, ground cover, and lawn. The landscape was not sculptured but was mature and had a graceful, old-fashioned feeling about it. It had been nurtured for all of the twentieth century, and that showed. It was a relaxing landscape. There were two rose gardens with older, fragrant varieties, through which the chickens navigated on their way to what was, for them, more hospitable surroundings.

All of the flower beds were fair game, although those that contained large flowering shrubs and bulbs were not often cultivated. Even though they were occasionally mulched and were watered during summer months, they were not as inviting to foraging chickens as the frequently cultivated beds containing annuals. Chickens rested under shrubs, but the soil there was not as soft for scratching as it was in the beds with such flowers as

delicate, easily destroyed impatiens and petunias.

Irrespective of location or plantings in flower beds, wherever the ground was soft, plants and lawn were vulnerable to large, scratching chicken feet with claws. The chickens were not welcome in any part of the yard, but keeping them away during

Shrubs bloomed from early spring until well into summer and early fall.

Of course if the chickens found a way into the vegetable garden, they preferred fresh tomatoes and lettuce to flowers, and if they managed to breach the netting, they decimated tender vegetables instead of delicate flowers. In fact if the day was hot, if the chickens were out, and if you didn't notice them heading toward a moist

The driveway back to the garage was also lined with flowering shrubs and trees.

hot summer days was like trying to force the tide back. The chickens kept returning, like waves forever rolling onto sandy beaches.

We tried anyway. When especially beautiful, fragile flowers and plants were at risk, the chickens were only allowed out in the mornings and were tricked into being closed in their chickenyard when they headed indoors to lay eggs, and then they were allowed out again in late afternoons. It was a ruthless tactic, but it really was the only solution until the most intense heat of summer had past.

flower bed at some point during the morning, you'd be well advised to check the vegetable garden.

As the flock grew in size, the chickens naturally fanned out more into places where they weren't welcome. More chickens meant more ground to cover. This was as much a function of their society and of each chicken's social status within it as it was a function of their insatiable need to scratch and devour delicate vegetables and to ravage flower gardens.

Once in a great while, those hens wanting to lay an egg in a nest that was already occupied by a more dominant hen, but finding themselves on the lowest end of the pecking order, began to explore the territory beyond the chicken house and chicken yard. Almost always they waited for their chance in The Nest Box, but one young hen in particular somehow found her own small nook away from the flock. It was in a very tiny, very narrow flower bed that ran just underneath one bank of the large living room windows. This small strip of soil with a few shrubs and annuals separated the outer wall of the house from the cement patio and framed that side of the living room.

The little nook chosen by this hen was up against the house and next to the kitchen door and steps. The door opened to the patio and the south side of the house, whereas the window above the kitchen sink overlooked the back yard on the north side of the house.

This hen must have been very shy and unassuming to actually leave the flock and make her way to her own little nest nearly every day, where she laid her egg. She was just beginning to lay and was scarcely more than a nervous juvenile. The place that she found couldn't have been any closer to the kitchen or her eggs more convenient to collect. You simply stepped outside the kitchen door.

The kitchen table was just inside the door. A large, low window looked out to the east, and the paned glass door looked south onto the patio. There was a screened door there too. When you were sitting at the kitchen table, you could see her through the east window, making her way from the back yard to the patio, and then you could see her through the kitchen door as she came to her little nest.

Every day she came to lay her egg, slowly, step by silent step, neck outstretched and listening for any danger. Her tension was palpable and extremely dramatic. She was out of sight of the flock and far, far away from it, and this was not normal for a chicken. She commanded our attention.

She generally arrived mid- to late morning. We didn't see her every day, but when there was time for a break and a cup of coffee at the kitchen table, we watched for her. She was always quiet and cautious, and sometimes she slipped past the side window and was around the corner before we noticed her.

We saw her again as she crept past the patio door, looking something like a heron in predator mode because her neck and bill were stretched out so far, and she gently settled herself into her own little nest. She was so careful that it took several minutes for her to pass by the east window and show up again on the patio, although the distance around that outside corner was only about ten feet.

This hen settled herself in the corner next to the kitchen door and steps.

Many times we spotted her only after she was nestled into her little corner of the world, and many times we simply found an egg there. We usually did not see her leave after she laid her egg, but that was no surprise because the few times we did see her leave, she was quiet but extraordinarily fast, swiftly making her way back to the flock, like an arrow whistling through space.

We had the sense from her general movements that this stage of uncertainty in her maturation process was a difficult stage and probably caused her great anxiety. Her body language spoke volumes.

When you noticed small but dramatic details about her daily appearance, you realized that she left the flock only out of dire necessity. As she grew older she eventually opted to lay her eggs in the chickenhouse. She must have learned how to assert herself forcefully enough to be able to use a nest box and was able to abandon her special nook. She seemed to be the only chicken that for a time laid eggs away from the chickenhouse. We missed watching her because her behavior was riveting, and she had a real flair for overkill, but the good news was that she didn't feel the need to leave the flock any more.

Chickens on the Back Stoop

The back door of the house opened from the back porch onto a small stoop, where in three or four steps you reached a sidewalk that led to the garage. As you walked to the garage, there was lawn on your right and the outer wall of old-garage-turned-multipurpose-room on your left. That back room shared a wall with the back porch and was accessed from within the porch, down a few steps to ground level. If you walked straight through the back porch, you went down those steps to the back room. If you turned right you went out the back door of the house, stood for a moment on the little stoop, then you turned left, went down a few steps and reached the sidewalk. Here the sidewalk was often flooded with warm sunlight on a cold day. The outer stucco wall of the back room held and reflected warmth, and there was very little wind. It was a wonderful place to bring chairs and a cup of tea.

After you passed the stucco wall, you crossed a breezeway to reach the garage. If you turned left and headed through the breezeway, you reached the large open area where the driveway ended. This was the front of the garage, where the wide open, inviting garage doors had led straight to the puppy food before it was moved. The other side of the back room, and its sliding glass doors, were on that side to your left.

However if you continued straight, a few steps later you arrived at the small door into the garage. The garage was essentially an elongated rectangle, car doors closer to the barn and shop and small door closer to the house.

Near the small door, to your immediate right, was the California bay laurel that had fallen during the heavy snowstorm. Continuing on to your right was the circular bed with jasmine, miniature roses, strawberry plants, and herbs, and that had been the luscious little glen with trillium before the tree fell. Then you came to the footbridge that led to the garden.

The chickens knew that breezeway well, because it was the path to many of their favorite places and led right to where you walked toward the back steps, the stoop, and the back door. Not only that, if the chickens were headed somewhere and used the breezeway to get there, you couldn't see them until they emerged from one side or the other. By now we realized that they were aware of this.

In early spring and late fall, and during some winter days, soil, lawn and flower beds were moist and chilly, but not the sidewalk and stoop. They were warm and dry when the sun was shining on them. The stucco wall there reflected the sun's warmth and stopped any windchill. This area was a protected place, perfect for soaking in rays from a wintry sun. It felt wonderful to stand there and relax in the warmth for a few moments.

Naturally then, there were times when you'd open the back door, head outside, and the door would bump into soft, feathered beings. The result was that you would leap up in the air so you wouldn't hurt a chicken, you might land precariously on a step, maybe lose your balance, and hold on for dear life to the pipe railing there. The chickens knew when they had a good spot, and they generally didn't scatter. They sometimes shuffled around a bit but unless you deliberately herded them away, they held their ground.

Just as they were quiet when they first reached the puppy food or when they found their way into the garden in summer months, they were quiet about making their way to the back stoop. Normally they visited among themselves when scratching and eating, wandering, looking around or relaxing somewhere, but they were silent when arranging themselves in the sunshine on the back stoop.

This was a small, fenced yard of ferns, azaleas, forget-me-nots, hawthorn, rhododendrons, and more. It was between the driveway and the house. This area was a chicken-free zone, but they never stopped looking for a way in.

As a result, their presence on the back stoop was always a surprise. Hopefully you weren't carrying a load of wash to the dryer in the garage, or an armful of anything to take anywhere, because you generally needed your hands and arms to grab the railing. Also, the stoop frequently needed to be hosed clean.

The chickens seemed to enjoy relaxing on the back stoop when they knew someone was in the kitchen close by. The kitchen was only a few steps away through the back porch. Over the kitchen sink was the large window that overlooked the back yard, but the window was too high to see any chickens on the back stoop. From the kitchen window, they were just outside, a few feet to the left, and down, conveniently hidden out of sight by the box protecting the water softener. You only saw the top half of the back door. Chickens rested comfortably out of sight and out of mind, until you tripped over them.

In warmer months the kitchen window was generally open. Once in a while, in spring and fall when the back stoop wasn't too warm from direct sun yet, but was still very nice on a chilly day, a soft chuckle or cooing could be heard near the kitchen window, the gentle sounds coming from the left, just out of sight.

If you were carrying leftover food, vegetable trimmings, fruit peelings or anything that might resemble promising pickings to a browsing chicken, and you headed out the back door to the garden to dig them into the already fertile soil, you were automatically besieged by chickens.

Chickens have a sharp sense of smell. When the kitchen window was open and they were drawing in the scent of a possible snack, it almost seemed that they watched and listened in case they could somehow snatch something to eat. If you were headed to the back door and they were aware of your mission, and they could and did figure this out, you were in danger of being ambushed.

They loved the back stoop, where they could soak up the sun on a chilly day.

As you thoughtlessly and happily stepped outside, they crowded around your feet and clucked insistently. No one wanted to hurt a chicken as they were small and round with soft feathers, so the best defense was a quick stepping action down the stairs and out into the garden. A shout at the chickens to scatter them generally resulted in small movements away for a split second, and then a stream of enthusiastic chickens followed you to the garden, just at your heels.

Digging the compost material into the garden soil had to be done with great efficiency. Otherwise in record time, it would quickly be scattered over a large area by opportunistic chickens, it would not compost quickly, and it was messy. You could step on apple peelings and wonder how they ever became so deeply embedded into the patterns on the soles of your shoes, and why they fell off so easily onto the carpet you'd just vacuumed.

If you assumed that the chickens were following their basic instinct for finding and eating food, this was true, but it was too easy to ignore the innate crafty nature of the flock. On the other hand, if you allowed your mind to appreciate the strategies they used when stalking you and your kitchen, and when enjoying the sun's warm rays in an off-limits area, you were astonished at the sheer consistency of their always turning up in the right place, at the right time.

Chapter 5

The Expanded Flock

The Silkies
Chicks With Their Own Bedroom
The Banty Mom
The Guineas

Time passed, and the chickens continued to cast their spell of enchantment over nearly everybody, although there were occasions when groans and shouts could be heard from the vegetable and flower gardens. The chickens were in their new house, and there was room for more. Not a lot more, just enough to bring their numbers up to around a dozen at any one time.

Neighbors received farm fresh brown eggs, and there were always plenty for the house. Fresh eggs are wonderful. They have firm whites and yolks, and they have a wholesome flavor that is not strong. If the chickens laying them are allowed to range, their eggs have firm, dark, tangerine-colored yolks from the fresh greens, yours, from your garden, often unplanned. If you need beaten egg whites, fresh egg whites become frothy and stiff in no time. You understand that your chicken-supplied food is natural and healthy.

The Silkies

It was time for hatching out little ones to replace older hens that passed on of old age. Introducing a few hens that were known to be good mothers helped with hatching out chicks, and Silkies are known to be excellent mothers. They did all the work. The Silkies incubated Rhode Island Red eggs and then diligently raised the little ones, protecting them and teaching them the infinite and eternal ways of chickendom.

There was an ulterior motive for choosing Silkies. They are a downy soft, round mass of the most delicate of feathers that fluff out around their little bodies like a dandelion head gone to seed. The impression was of a soft halo of feathers walking around on two feathered legs and feet. Their short combs, tongues and feet were bluish grey but everything else was basically a gently rippling white, round mass. There was no way you could not adore a Silky.

Since there were walnut drying shelves facing each other on the walls of the chickenhouse as there were in the rest of the barn, the free shelf not holding nests and roosts for the main flock became the nursery shelf. The chickens didn't really use it anyway.

It was screened off at its edge, and a small door was constructed at one side. The shelf itself was about thirty inches off the ground floor, and the large area beneath it was still available to the flock if anybody wanted it. Most members of the flock were only interested in their home's open and roomy middle area with their feeder and waterer, and the shelf with their nest boxes. Food and sleep.

The two shelves, the areas beneath the two shelves, and the middle area always had soft pine shavings laid down for the comfort of the inhabitants, who rarely made

use of all the space they had. Space lost to a nursery was not a problem.

On the screened-off shelf, strong and comfortable nest boxes were arranged with shims under one end to level them. The shelves weren't severely slanted, but slanted just enough so walnuts would roll down after drying, for collecting at the front edge. The nest boxes for the brooding hens were roomy, filled with pine shavings and partially open at the front. This allowed privacy for the hen, important because broody hens are on alert so their future chicks remain safe from anything that comes too close for comfort. Overall it was a spacious area but not so large that little chicks would ever be very far from their mothers.

This seemed to be a good arrangement. The Silkies had their privacy, and yet they were still inside the chickenhouse, in contact with other, albeit much larger, chickens. The outer door of the chicken house was closed and latched every night, so everyone including Silkies was safe inside. In the nursery area, the Silkies' feeder and waterer were close to the food and water supply. These small, apparently delicate chickens were warm, dry and off the ground. They seemed to be happy and at peace in their shelf home.

A hen setting on eggs is well aware of her environment and of each little thing in it, including curious onlookers. Whenever their area was checked, feeders filled and water changed, the Silkies watched every single move with baleful eyes and hunched down and spread themselves out over their eggs even more than usual. If your hand strayed too close to the opening of a nest box, a hard bill nailed you, with force. In the blink of an eye those soft, downy Silkies became warrior chickens.

A few days before chicks began to hatch, the Silkies grew even more serious about spreading their feathers over the soon-to-be new chicks. The Silkies didn't move, not even a feather. They actually looked statuesque, or perhaps petrified. They probably grabbed a bite to eat and a sip of water on the run, but that didn't happen at a time when anyone was looking. They were too protective to leave the nest when others were around.

Then one morning there were the sounds of tiny cheeps emanating from within the mothers' soft, fluffed bodies. It was best not to disturb them, as baby chicks didn't always hatch simultaneously. You didn't want the mother hen to leave the nest, thinking that all the babies had already hatched out. She needed to care for the cheeping babies and hatching newborns. They had to be kept very warm, as hypothermia was deadly for them.

You also had to provide a little feeder with baby chick food that they could actually reach, since they were very tiny. You provided a small waterer for them as well. Baby chicks explored their surroundings and climbed into waterers at times, and they needed to be able to climb out again. It was absolutely necessary to have safe and appropriate feeders and waterers in the nursery.

After a few days of hearing soft peeping in and around the Silkies, you saw tiny yellow, fuzzy heads peeking out between soft Silky feathers. The babies peered out from under wings, through wings, between feathered feet, and anywhere there was a place to stay warm and at the same time peek out at the world.

By that time, with their babies in tow, the Silkies were venturing out to food and water. These trips were quick, and along the way there was down time, when the Silkies hunched down and spread out their feathers, looking a little like they were wearing southern ballroom gowns that fluffed out all around them as they crouched. Baby chicks scurried and pried their way into the mass of feathers to settle down for safety, warmth, and a nap.

As the days wore on, the little families spent more and more time away from the nests around their shelf home, although they always returned to cozy nests for the night. Eventually the chicks grew so large that the Silkies could no longer spread their feathers far enough to cover them all.

This seemed to be the beginning of the time when the Silkies began to gradually wean the babies. By this time, the chicks had lost many, if not most, of their down feathers and were growing the rust colored feathers of adult birds, although they were still very small compared to adult Rhode Island Reds.

Eventually the chicks ran around more on their own than with their surrogate mothers. They quickly became gangly, long-legged adolescents with their true plumage. They were removed from the nursery and stayed in a group to themselves in an interim home, a half-way house.

Then they began to fill out, resembling slender adult chickens after about six months. By then they had become members of the main flock although until they started to lay, they stayed close together and were on the bottom of the pecking order.

The little Silkies had worked their magic, and they complacently settled into a life of contented eating and murmuring quietly among themselves. They were too small to be allowed into the main flock. It wasn't safe to be outside as a brilliant white, movable snack, or to take part in pecking order jostling involving chickens at least twice their size. When they weren't nesting, their nature was gentle and calm. Their nature plus their diminutive size put them at a disadvantage with regard to the Rhode Island Red hierarchy.

They had swept us into their friendly, kindly, and beautifully feathered world. It was simply wrong to not let them have a group of their own. So the numbers of Silkies increased. Their number didn't increase by much, but a few more joined the snowy white Silkies.

A chickenyard within the main chickenyard was constructed. First, a small ramp allowed the Silkies to descend from their shelf to the newly fenced-in ground floor beneath it. We simply ran chicken wire from the edge of the shelf to the floor and fastened it to simple framework.

The Silkies headed outside through a small opening in the outer wall, leading to their own personal chickenyard. It was not large, but it was a nice yard for them. Its top was about four feet off the ground, covered with chicken wire. Thus the small condo and yard were completely enclosed for the safety of the sweet-natured little chickens.

There was a Silky rooster among them now and little Silkies began to arrive. They included multicolored variations of the adults, but most were white. Silky chicks had yellow down but when they began to grow their fine, delicate feathers, they looked like tiny, furry marshmallows scampering about. They moved surprisingly fast on their little feathered legs.

Meanwhile the Rhode Island Reds went about their business as usual, mostly ignoring the fuzzy additions to their home. They took everything in their stride. As always, their society endured, and when you did something that you thought could cross their societal boundaries, it often turned out to be inconsequential to them. They were a flock unto themselves.

The Silkies' house was constructed from space that the Reds had hardly used, and the Silkies' yard took relatively little space. In fact the Rhode Island Reds enjoyed hopping up on the posts that were the framework for the small yard, where they thoughtfully looked out toward the vegetable garden and across the orchard.

It was true. You existed as an addendum to the chickens. They lived in the same general environment as you did, but they belonged to no one.

Chicks With Their Own Bedroom

When the little Rhode Island Red chicks lost their downy fluff and grew feathers, but were still too small to merge with the flock of adults, they had to have another place to grow. They still needed warmth, but even a small group of them was too much for a petite Silky hen to nurture. It was unfair to ask that of the gentle-natured little hens, who frantically tried to stuff overly large babies back under their wings. The best and only place for the babies appeared to be in the back room of the house.

Obviously they had to be contained, so a very large, very strong cardboard box was secured. It had tall sides that were taped at the corners to prevent sagging, and the result was a nice, captive home for the young babies. Shavings covered the bottom of the box. On one side an electrical socket with along neck was thrust through an opening just large enough for it to fit snugly, and was taped securely in place. A very low wattage light bulb was added, with the result that the bulb was at least a few inches into the box, away from any sides, high enough to be left undisturbed by the chicks, and yet low enough to provide the warmth that they needed. This was tricky, because you didn't want any chance of a problem from electricity or from chicks. When everything was properly positioned and secured well, it worked. But you still checked it several times a day, and you wished that you'd had the foresight to have a real brooder on hand.

This cat had arrived several years earlier. He achieved the name Peril, weighed about twenty pounds, and bowed to no one. Here he was resting about fifteen feet from where the baby chicks stayed when they were there.

A small wooden platform a few inches high was positioned in one corner, and a small feeder and waterer were placed there. The platform had to be short enough for small chicks to climb up for food and water, but tall enough to keep out shavings that the chicks had a tendency to scatter, since they scampered all around their enclosure.

Every week or so, the platform had to be replaced with one a bit higher, as the chicks grew taller and even more active, sending shavings into anything and everything. Every few weeks the warming bulb had to be repositioned to a higher location, and the box had to be replaced with a larger one.

Meanwhile, the dogs and the cat lived both inside and outside. They had to learn that the babies could be seen but not touched. After a few misunderstandings the dogs enjoyed socializing with the chicks, watching them for hours. However, the very large cat had to be monitored. He could have easily made off with dinner with only a flick of one large, well-clawed paw. He was not a shy cat and was often on the prowl when he was outside, although he received at least his share of food every day. He was a wonderful, affectionate cat, but he was assertive.

Eventually whatever covered about half of the top of the box and helped keep the occupants warm was removed for good. Shortly thereafter, if you were lucky and it was warm enough outside, you allowed the now juvenile chickens to join the flock. Their cardboard home was discarded.

This was a difficult time for them. They seemed to be large enough, having almost learned how to escape their cardboard box, and desperately needed more space that was actually designed for chickens. But they were still small to a group of adult hens. If the timing worked out just right they were assimilated, sort of, into the main flock, although they remained together as a small group. If they were a little too small, they were chased away by adult hens for whom they were underfoot, small nuisances that looked for food that their elders wanted.

At times a few juveniles wandered too close to a few adult hens, and the adults pecked at them, essentially shoving them to the very bottom of the pecking order. There were no physical wounds, but the surprise and apparently hurt feelings resulted in cries and sudden loud squeaks that shattered peaceful surroundings.

Enter Sarge. He didn't like to hear calls of distress from anybody, not even from juvenile chickens. He ran to the rescue every time, taking in the situation when he arrived on scene. He clucked loudly and resolutely stalked about, not allowing any hen to bother the half grown chickens and keeping the young ones in a herd. No one, but no one, made another chicken squeal, unless that someone was Sarge himself.

If the weather was cool and the chicks still required extra heat, they moved into the area under the nursery ledge that had been their first home. A very low wattage light bulb for warmth was very, very carefully arranged on the inside of the chickenhouse, square in the middle of the chicken wire, well away from any wood, or shavings, or nest box, or ramp. This was tense because you automatically thought about the old barn, and you really wished you'd purchased a large brooder, even though you were replacing flock members, not selling chickens. Or so you rationalized. The young juveniles remained in this area for about two or three weeks, until they no longer needed the warmth of the light bulb and were ready to begin their assimilation into the main flock. Sarge took it from there.

One way or another and sometimes in stages, young chickens were gradually integrated into the flock at large. It wasn't long before they were scurrying about underfoot and beginning to behave just like the adults. They had become bona fide members of the flock even though they were still at the very lowest rung of the pecking order.

The Banty Mom

After the Silkies arrived and began to incubate their own eggs, a black Banty hen joined the Silkies in the nursery area. She wasn't any larger than they were. Her feathers weren't Silky soft like theirs but were thick and glossy blue-black. She was a very diminutive, solid black chicken with a small, bright red comb. Her personality blended well with the Silkies' personalities, as she was soft spoken and cordial like they were. Theirs was a small, friendly way of living, like an eternal, peaceful afternoon gathering of friends enjoying a pleasant game of bridge and sharing tea and crumpets. Some Banties are feisty and very quick on their feet, but she was extremely even-tempered and wandered about in a contented fashion, chuckling quietly along with the Silkies.

It turned out that she was also an excellent mother hen. She eyed any nest box with more than one egg in it as a potential home with family, and considered settling in to hatch out whatever was there. When she was nesting, she included eggs of all sizes. It didn't matter to her. They were pure potential and she was there to see them hatch, and then to protect them.

She was fascinating. From the time she found herself within the proximity of a nest box with an egg or two, it seemed to take only a few moments until it looked like she was wondering about hoarding the eggs and settling herself into the nest box. She didn't care whose nest box it might be, and she was not possessive at that point, not yet. She just carefully watched the cache of eggs.

When she decided to settle in, a free nest box was located conveniently close to the feeder and waterer, because once settled, she would not leave the eggs for more than a few moments at most. Her nest box was filled with new, fresh pine shavings, and carefully placed into it were only enough eggs for her to comfortably manage. She always found this nest box very quickly, claimed it for her own, and settled down to incubate the eggs.

The Silkies might have been busy raising a brood of their own, or more likely were enjoying quiet time within the safety of their communal home. The Silkies and the black Banty were not allowed to hatch out chicks too often because it didn't seem healthy for them. Their metabolism seemed to change when they were incubating eggs, because they were capable of not moving for very long periods of time, and they ate ravenously but not often. During the time when the chicks began to hatch, the hens were extremely focused on staying still and protecting the new downy chicks from any perceived danger. They were on high red alert.

When the little black hen's chicks hatched, as usual after a day or so they began to venture out of the nest box in search of food and water, but only for a few moments at a time. The little black hen moved slowly and carefully with them, showing them where to eat and where to drink. She appeared to be a little stiff for those first few days, but when you tried to hold a tiny baby and exclaim over it, the stiffness vanished. She ran at you like a roadrunner, her bill outstretched.

It was always wise to position the small chick feeder and waterer very close to the new family, so food and water were readily available. You wanted chicks to eat and drink as much as they needed, and at first they were too tiny to wander very far. This meant that when filling the feeder and providing fresh water, your hand regularly came in close proximity to their home. You had to be very careful and very quick if you wanted to avoid being pecked.

Any waterer that was too large for the babies was removed from the nursery because once chicks began to explore, they ran everywhere within their home area, and they got into everything. They were happy, playful and curious little creatures, and they needed protection from just about anything, including water that was too deep for them.

The black hen never forgot this. She constantly clucked in a rhythmic fashion, in a very clear and projecting voice that brought the chicks to abrupt attention and

called them to her. She kept them in an orderly group this way. Whenever one or two strayed too far away, she called and they came to her. They recognized the tone.

It seemed like this little Banty felt that she could never do enough for the chicks. She indulged in overkill. If they were Silky chicks, she was able to raise them to adolescence or to a time when they gradually became more naturally independent. If they were Rhode Island Red chicks, they grew to a point where it was difficult for her to care for them because they were too large, although she never gave up trying. To protect her and to keep her sane, it was necessary to remove them to a warm box or another area in summer months, so they could continue to grow.

This event had to be carefully timed. The ideal time to remove them was just about when the little hen herself realized that she couldn't keep them warm, because they were too large. She could scarcely keep up with them because their legs were so much longer than hers were. They were scampering here and there, running farther and farther away from her. She grew steadily more upset and frazzled.

This was just about the perfect time to remove them. Of course she mourned their loss, but she was so tired she quickly collapsed into a state of soft chuckling, fluffing herself in deep shavings and eating, making up for meals skipped so she could teach her chicks to eat rather than feed herself. She needed the rest. She was such a responsible hen that you couldn't allow her to raise chicks very often, because her process was too hard on her little system.

The little black hen, the best mother of all, was overrun with juvenile Silkies. She was a very patient mother.

Even though whispery soft Silkies and the extremely sweet natured black Banty hen had their own personalities apart from the Rhode Island Reds, and even apart from each other, they were still chickens. Theirs were the ways of all chickendom. The basic process of chick rearing seemed to be uniform among all chickens and was always nice to observe, but it was a pleasure just to be acquainted with Silkies and with the black Banty, even if they never hatched and raised clutches of chicks.

Just as was the case with the main flock, they led their own structured lives within their own structured society, and so did their chicks. You were neither welcome nor unwelcome in their world. However you were definitely a threat whenever you or your hand came too close to their babies for comfort.

The Guineas

Some time after the chickens had moved into their new home on the eastern side of the barn, with its exposure to the morning sun, and after the Silkies were in residence, Guinea fowl joined the expanding flock. They were supposed to be rather fierce toward snakes and other invading wildlife, and were supposed to be a ready-made, natural alarm system.

After the unwelcome dog had come and gone, and after rattlesnakes had visited a few too many times during a dry summer, a natural alarm system that moved about with the chickens was a good idea. A small group of Guineas came to live in the chickenhouse and chickenyard, after we were assured that they would not create problems for the Rhode Island Reds. We considered them to be a safety feature for the flock in general. They were truly unusual and unique, beautiful in their own way.

Guinea fowl are protective of territory and have an extremely loud and piercing cry that is almost painful to the ears when the birds are calling in good form. If you were standing close to them and they began calling an alarm, you were forced to cover your ears. They certainly helped to alert all of us to any intruders, and sure enough, we didn't see rattlesnakes after they arrived.

They stayed together in a small group, not really intermingling with the chickens, and ranging further out and around the chickenhouse and chickenyard than the chickens themselves did. If they saw something unusual, they stared at it and then went into alarm mode. When they were relaxed, they ranged and peacefully foraged, all together, in a tight bundle.

They were intriguing to watch, not least because they had an unusual appearance due to the horn-like protrusion on top of their heads. Their heads were not feathered, and toward the sides, behind their bills, they had red, firm wattles that protruded out more than down. They were otherwise sleek and rounded in appearance with a bone structure more delicate than chickens, and they were shades of grey or white with small, regular, white spots all over their bodies. They looked as though they were wearing a very finely-crafted suit of little white polka-dots against a charcoal or lighter grey backdrop. Through the years there were one or two that were solid dark grey with a lavender sheen, and one or two that were white.

They also ran very fast and flew very well. No one in the chickenhouse or chickenyard had clipped wings, and the Guineas were free to fly into trees if they

Even though Sarge was alert as always, the guineas watched too, just outside the chickenyard.

wished, although they generally wandered about on the ground. They preferred to sleep inside with the chickens, but even at night they roosted together in a small, round, polka-dot bundle.

Guinea society seemed to be less overtly aggressive within itself than chicken society appeared to be. At least on the surface, Guineas exhibited more equality among themselves and had a less stringent pecking order. However, it was possible that we didn't recognize the finer points of their communications with one another. There did seem to be a leader of sorts. This was generally a Guinea hen that was often older and more experienced than the others.

Like the chickens, they seemed to accept that we were living in the same general area as they were. They were basically unconcerned about us, and they didn't impose. Perhaps this was because they didn't have such large feet and didn't scratch quite so vigorously as chickens scratched. They didn't seem to decimate delicate flowers and vegetables with quite the happy abandon that chickens did. But they did like fresh vegetables, especially ripe tomatoes which they pierced and left, like chickens did. They loved relaxing in soft grass, but they seemed to be gentler with it than chickens were. The grass actually remained intact.

They were not pretentious and seemed to go about their daily lives with a certain quiet humility, until they sounded their alarm. Then they were truly impressive. They were altogether a pleasant addition, and we treasured and appreciated them.

We had the impression that these Guineas were less domesticated than chickens were. However if you looked, really looked, at chicken society you understood that chickens carefully adhered to their own ways, and our assumption about their being completely domesticated by our species wasn't entirely warranted. Chickens come in many sizes, shapes and colors within the world of chickendom, but chicken society is simply chicken society, and we're only along for the ride. If you figured that chickens and other fowl were domestic in that our species cultivated them for eggs and for southern fried for instance, then yes, they were domestic. In their unassuming manner, Guineas seemed to be even more independent of our species than chickens were.

When dusk fell, you always hoped that the Guineas were already in the chickenhouse for the night, or were on their way there. They became easily frightened and completely disoriented when there was almost no daylight left. If you tried to herd them into the chickenhouse and it was a little too dark, they tended to panic and run. They didn't seem to know where they were running, but they kept running anyway, and when they stopped they could be far, far away from home because they traveled fast.

When morning came, if they had survived nocturnal predators and if they weren't too far away, you could hear them calling to one another, and the lost souls returned. But there was always the danger that they were gone for good. A much better idea was to nudge them toward the chickenhouse at the end of the day, when the chickens were headed inside and there was still ample light. This was only necessary when a few foraged a little too far afield and didn't notice that most of their little group was heading in for the night.

None of the small group that lived with us succumbed to predators or ran away for good, but there were a few times when wayward Guineas kept us nervous and worried. Not long after their arrival we learned to help the Guineas into

The little group was taking in the sun on a winter day.

the chickenhouse when it seemed wise, but maybe in reality they were more able to care for themselves than we knew.

One day, dusk approached and a Guinea hen became a little frantic because she had lagged behind, and everyone else was indoors for the night. She was outside the chickenyard fence and was too upset to find the door into the chickenyard. When I walked around behind her and gently tiptoed toward her to encourage her to round the far corner and find the door, she veered away and took off over the creek, heading out into the orchard, running as fast as her little legs could carry her. She was skimming over the ground.

Meanwhile the little Aussie puppy had matured into an adult. He spent time outside the chickenyard fence, feeling protective of the inhabitants within. Apparently he figured that the Guinea hen needed to be herded into the chickenyard and the safety of the chickenhouse, and he couldn't accept watching her run away. He sprinted after her, running hard. When she dodged in full flight, he dodged in full pursuit. After several hundred feet of chasing her, he finally caught her and waited there for me to reach them both, to carry her back to the chickenhouse.

I had never seen him run after a bird that way and frankly didn't know what to expect. When I reached them, he was holding her in his mouth just firmly enough to keep her still, but she didn't have a scratch or even a ruffled feather. This was amazing since at first she had truly struggled, and Guineas are surprisingly strong for their size. She was still frightened but was hunched down and still, although if the grip holding her had lessened even a trifle, she probably would have tried to make a dash for it. Apparently he figured that she was part of the herd that he existed to watch and protect.

It was nearly dark and there had recently been coyotes nearby, so with considerable relief I carefully carried her back to the chickenhouse, where she was safe. When you are holding a bird and you allow it to balance itself, and you speak soothingly and very gently rub the back of its head with one or two finger tips, sometimes the bird relaxes, although I don't know specifically why. By the time we were back at the chickenhouse, she was quiet. This harrowing experience must have done something to her psyche because after that time, she stayed closer to home, like the chicken that swam.

A few years after the Guineas had arrived we saw them in real action. An unsuspecting dog was in the orchard. It was another neighbor's dog, and apparently it had never seen Guineas before and didn't quite understand what they were. As it wandered closer to the foraging chickens, the Guineas arranged themselves in a single straight line between dog and chickens, a few feet apart from one another. Calling that ear splitting alarm cry that they had, they slowly and steadily advanced toward the hapless dog. They marched onward. The dog cowered and retreated.

They didn't stop until the dog was backed well into a neighboring orchard. Then they stopped, still in a straight line and still spaced equally apart from one another, and they continued their alarm until the dog was far, far away. They appeared to settle down and relax a little, and began to make their way back to the chickens, foraging as they came.

An army couldn't have handled the unfortunate dog any better than the Guineas had. The dog did not return. The Guineas' successful maneuver was outstanding.

They didn't mind floodwaters over the culvert behind the
chickenyard. There were worms and bugs there.

Chapter 6

The Menagerie

The Bear Tracks
The Rat Spring
The Rattlesnake Summer
The Skunk Feast
The Neighborhood Dogs
The Mallard Pair
The Huge Gopher Snake
The Coyotes
The Oblivious Chickens

The general neighborhood in which the chickens lived was rural, with farmlands and hills that rose in elevation as they extended back into an area of national forest. Wildlife was everywhere, although not normally at your back door. However, as it turned out, the creek that ran along the side of the barn was a very old waterway that had once been a much larger creek. Most of it had been re-routed by farmers about a century before, but much of the original watershed drained into this little creek.

Wildlife doesn't forget ancient pathways, and this creek was no exception. Many animals made their way down the creek in summer, because it led to a rich wetland area that had once been more expansive and part of a large, natural marshland and lake. During the hot, dry summer, you could find water and food in an area like this, and you continued to follow traditional routes just as your parents and their parents before them had done, when they taught their offspring how to survive. There were tracks everywhere along the sides of the creek and in its bed during summer, until the ground became too dry and too hard.

Naturally where there is water and food, there is life, and if you were a microbe, an insect, an invertebrate, a mammal, a bird, or whatever, if you were looking for food, chances were good that you could find it along the creek and in the wetland area. If you were a deer you could easily cross the orchards to the creek, where you could enjoy a refreshing drink of water and browse along the banks where grass and herbivorous plants were plentiful. If you were a squirrel, you first of all found left over walnuts in the

orchard, but the creek promised more, since walnuts tended to roll down its sides. If you were a predator of some size, you could find many meals along the creek. These meals potentially included chickens.

The Bear Tracks

Several distinctive tracks along the side of the creek were those of a small bear. These tracks were visible very close to the back of the barn. This particular bear had visited the area long before the chickens arrived, and locals had long since tried to trap it and release it further back into the hills. Apparently it came too close to people's homes for their comfort, and at least once during springtime, she was observed accompanied by cubs. It was altogether best for her and her family, for people, their pets, and their livestock if she could be relocated to a safer environment. Rumor had it that she had been moved once before but had returned to the area.

Her tracks were easy to see, in the mud along the sides of the creek, in the pear orchard way out behind the barn, and near the creek next to the hills. She feasted on ripe and tasty pears missed during the harvest and on those that accidentally fell to the ground and ripened there. When harvest was over, the pear orchards were quiet and comfortable for her. Dusk was not the best time to walk back in the pear orchard, as dusk seemed to be around her dinnertime. She was occasionally observed around that time of day, moving here and there in the pear orchard and munching away. Apparently her experience at having once been captured and moved had made her wary, since ever after, she was able to avoid pursuers and was notoriously cunning about outwitting them. Because she left her tracks behind, it was easy to know when she was nearby and when to be on the lookout for her.

Shortly after we moved to the area, a friend visited and brought his red-boned hound, Pie. Pie went everywhere with him. She was a sweet-natured dog and enjoyed stretching into a good run when out in the orchard, heading away and circling back to us. She was an active and curious dog.

One pleasant evening, well before dusk, we were walking along the creek where it ran along the base of a hill. We were headed toward more hills and away from civilization. We were relaxed and were enjoying the balmy air, when Pie became interested in something about half-way up the side of the hill nearest to us. She broke into a dead run, her nose stretched out in front of her, baying soulfully as she ran up the hillside.

The little bear broke into a run also, crashing through the underbrush along the hillside, heading farther into the hills away from civilization, with Pie on her heels, at least as near as we could tell.

Like a peninsula, these hills extended out into the basin that was our neighborhood, and for many long centuries, had been the floodplain of the nearby lake. We could and did flood on occasion. About an eighth of a mile farther back there was a sort of saddleback in the silhouette of the hills.

If you crossed over the top of the saddleback and walked down the peninsula along its opposite side, you came to the edge where it gave way to the basin, you rounded the tip, and you headed back along the side where we happened to be walking. We weren't on a hill but were at the base of one, beside the creek that wound around it.

The little bear crossed the saddleback, ran along the other side of the hill, rounded its end and came back toward us. She was no fool. She was running in a large, elongated circle with a baying, panting Pie fairly close on her heels, if our ears were hearing it right. We thought we saw them both go by the first time around, following a trail that was probably a deer trail. We heard them fade into the distance, then we heard them coming back, but on the other side of the hill, we thought, and we listened for their progress. As near as we could tell, we thought we heard them coming

There was a bit of a saddleback in the line of hills.

85

back toward us again, on our side. From what we could figure out, this time the bear had managed a significant lead. When she came to a place on the hillside not far from where we were, we saw where movement in the brush stopped, we saw the brush move above the trail, and then we only heard Pie.

She was focused and followed her nose along that trail, right past where we thought the bear might be. We didn't see what happened after that because whatever was there remained very quiet, but it seemed to us that Pie ran the circle again, or at least ran around a lot of brushy area, before she grew exhausted and confused enough to stop and come back to us. Most of us cheered for the little bear. We felt enormous respect for her and compassion for Pie too, after we stopped laughing.

The chickens arrived about a year later. When they moved into their first home in the back corner of the barn, there was some concern for their safety from this bear. Sure enough, not long after their arrival, there were bear tracks in the mud along the creek, coming from the direction of the hills and milling around the area behind the barn. But there was never an indication that the bear actually tried to find a way to reach the chickens. She investigated their presence every spring for a few years, but otherwise she didn't bother them. Then one spring there were no more bear tracks. We heard that she had finally been captured, again, and this time she had been transported deep into the neighboring national forest and released there. It was a happy outcome for her as she was much safer there, but the plain truth was that we missed her.

This bay laurel and underbrush were directly across the creek, on the hillside. Part of the great chase happened through here.

The Rat Spring

There were other animals that walked and crawled around the barn, the vegetable garden, the yards, and the orchard, in addition to the bear and other wildlife drawn to the creek, living in it, and flying over it. But rats did not come to mind until one day, they simply appeared.

At first there were only a few, darting quickly from shadow to shadow in the depths of the old barn. It was natural that a rat or two would inhabit the barn, because it had dark corners and places where they could live quietly, undetected. But the timing was the clue. They were first spotted a few days after huge amounts of blackberry vines were cleared from the sides of the creek across the road, a good thing.

After the creek went through a culvert under the road, it turned first right, then left, and then ran on toward the seasonal wetlands. All along the creek, and all around the edges of the wetland, grew large, lush stands of tangled blackberry vines. They were full of succulent, sweet fruit around July, but they also choked the edges of the creek and tended to impede winter runoff. One summer, neighbors who owned this land cleared them out. Their roots remained to live and sprout another year, although thereafter they were kept in check and never reached the same size and mass.

That same summer, a huge, long, vacant, old cannery building about a quarter of a mile away was partially dismantled. It had originally been constructed in the early part of the twentieth century for processing locally grown green beans, but by now it was very old and mostly shabby. Its timbers were enormous and beautiful, testaments to solid construction and to old growth lumber from the local area, milled at the local mill.

The old cannery was located along a larger creek. It was what had come into being late in the previous century when local farmers re-routed most of the channel of what was now our little creek. Our little creek had been a very large creek for thousands of years, its watershed reaching well into the mountains of the national forest.

Our little creek, running along the base of the hills nearest us, through the orchards, and near the side of the barn, was all that remained of the original broad, relatively shallow channel. The farmers cut the new channel away from

The re-routed channel carried serious amounts of runoff in winter.

the base of the hills where it had spread out, and they forced it into a more or less straight line toward the lake. It didn't meander on its way there any more, and they were able to plow the rich floodplain soils.

The new channel was much larger and carried significant amounts of water in winter and spring. It was banked by mounds of blackberries and willow, and generally had running water during hot summer months. If you were a rat, the huge, abandoned cannery building with its dark corners, nooks and crannies, and nearby blackberry thickets, plus fresh water, must have been inviting.

About midway through the twentieth century levees were constructed along the larger creek to control its flooding, keeping water more or less confined to the creek. According to those who had experienced pre-levee floodwaters, water was not very deep and was patchy across much of the floodplain. Thus, older homes were built above water levels. Unfortunately, during a few later years with unusually heavy, unexpected runoff, levees overtopped, and floodwaters were not as shallow. We live and learn.

Meanwhile the old abandoned cannery building that didn't really flood became an even more attractive home for rats. During that fateful time, when the building was dismantled near the large creek and blackberry vines were removed from the small creek, untold numbers of rats naturally dispersed outward, seeking new homes.

It was nearly springtime and there was the old barn, dry, warm, and empty except for the chickens. Where there had been no rats, suddenly a few were seen and were heard scurrying around. A deceased rat was taken to the local department of agriculture. The local agricultural commissioner came out to see the barn for himself.

He walked around it during daylight hours and stated, with a relaxed and bemused expression, that because a few rats were seen in the daylight, there were in actuality probably a few thousand rats inhabiting it. If you came out at night and walked through the barn with a flashlight pointing at various ledges, he said, you'd probably see solid lines of rats staring back at you. He said that these were Norway rats and that he hadn't seen them in the county before. However, rats are hardy and quiet, and they were probably in many more places than was generally assumed. Anyway, he authorized purchase of bait for them.

No one came out to the barn at night. You didn't want to see thousands of pairs of eyes shining at you from ledges over your head. Eliminating a large mass of rats was truly an awful thought, but the situation regarding potential disease called for drastic measures. We used that barn and needed to keep it disease free. The chickens slept in that barn. Their house was in that barn, and their health was important. Their food had always been in tight metal containers, but they themselves were dead weight slumbering through the night, and they didn't need furry visitors. Extra items that were in storage and walnuts gleaned after the main harvest were also in that barn.

The agricultural commissioner suggested a plan for bait stations made from old tires. These were made in such a way that other animals, like chickens, couldn't be harmed. They were carefully placed behind the barn, in locations chosen with consideration for safety of wildlife and chickens. These stations had to be checked daily, and deceased rats in and around the barn had to be collected and destroyed. This went on for a few months. It turned out that the agricultural commissioner was right when he said there were probably thousands in that barn.

Eventually fewer and fewer rats were found, and when a few weeks went by and no rats, dead or alive, were discovered, it was time to clean the barn, a truly daunting task. Very old, long and loose clothing covered other old clothes, protective masks covered noses, and brooms were used to sweep out the entire barn. Whatever could be destroyed in the burn barrel was dumped there, and it was in constant use for several days. Thank goodness burn barrels were still allowed at that time.

The only place that didn't need such strenuous cleaning was the chickenhouse. That wasn't because the chickenhouse didn't need to be thoroughly cleaned after the rats were gone, but rather because their house had never become very dirty, and rat droppings were not found there, although we didn't know why. We knew the chickens chased mice, but rats were considerably larger than mice. We gave the chickenhouse a thorough cleaning anyway.

After the dust had settled, the barn was completely swept again, and finally the last

The burn barrel was conveniently located just
behind the barn, at a safe distance.

step was to mix a strong bleach solution in a sprayer and spray down the entire barn. It needed to be really soaked, chickenhouse included.

On the day planned for this, in early morning, the chickenhouse was stripped of everything including chickens that cheerfully headed outside for the day. Food, water, and a few cleaned boxes were just outside their door. All surfaces including nest boxes were cleaned and sprayed straight away so they would be thoroughly dry by evening, and hopefully the odor of strong bleach solution would dissipate well before dusk. Then we went to work on the barn itself.

After the chickenhouse dried, fresh food and fresh water were placed in clean containers, and fresh shavings were liberally spread in clean nest boxes, on clean floors and on clean ledges. When they trooped in for the night, the chickens made their way through mounds of fresh pine shavings to dinner in newly scrubbed feeders, and then they hopped up onto to their ledge, settling in for the night. They were unimpressed.

They didn't seem to be affected one way or another by the onslaught of rats that particular spring. We were very definitely affected, but true to form, the chickens were only curious onlookers to a drama that didn't directly have anything to do with them.

Finally the barn was clean, disinfected, and rat-free. We were all in good shape, which frankly surprised us, although there were huge white blotches and holes in clothing and a few light patches of hair, where it had escaped the cloth wrappings we'd used. Early summer was here. Over time, a few rats moved in and lived in deep, dark recesses of the barn, but thereafter their numbers were kept under control, and the rat spring was finally over. Everybody breathed a huge sigh of relief.

Not until the old barn was dismantled many years later were more rats observed. By that time the chickens had moved with us to a house a few orchards away. The barn had been leaning more and more for a very long time, but one year it began to move in earnest. It creaked more, and bits of rubble began to slide out of the upstairs opening. As it moved, you began to see very long square nails on the ground alongside it. In fact you had to stay alert in case it ejected more nails at you as you walked by.

Board by board, the old barn was dismantled before it actually keeled over. First the tin roof was removed, then the siding, and finally the framework. All the wonderful old lumber was saved, the roofing was saved, and quite a few square nails were saved too.

The dismantling process didn't happen overnight. As more and more of the barn was taken apart, rats began to emerge. No one had believed that their numbers had significantly increased since the rat spring, but everyone was wrong, although populations never came anywhere close to the original infestation. Still, early each evening rats emerged in small groups from the back of the barn into the open, and as mentioned earlier, for some the social event of the evening was to gather behind the barn with chairs and twenty-twos, eliminating rats.

The Rattlesnake Summer

Generations upon generations of wildlife knew that not only did the creek beside the barn promise water throughout most of the year, but also that its dry bed in summer was a superhighway to seasonal wetlands, ponds and a lake. After all, it was an ancient waterway. During summer months, wildlife of all kinds naturally traveled down the creek bed seeking water. They knew instinctively that this was the right thing to do. However, homes had been built in more recent times, and animals reached the barn and the house before they reached marshland. The vegetable garden, the yard, sprinklers, spigots and pipes meant that water was around somewhere, and animals were aware of that. It was just a matter of finding where the water could be accessed.

One late morning during a coffee break, we noticed movement across the creek. At first we didn't see clearly what was moving, but then a mother skunk followed by her four offspring, all in single file, came into full view. They were walking with some determination along the other side of the creek, following it faithfully toward the road. The creek was completely dry, and they continued on through the culvert under the road, climbed back to the top of the creek bank on the other side again, and went on their way toward the marshlands. It appeared they were headed to summer digs.

During another summer that was especially hot and dry, there were rumors that rattlesnakes were out and about earlier than usual. Normally rattlesnakes didn't bother anybody around the barn, house and garden. They were probably around now and then but were quiet and remained unseen. You nevertheless watched where you stepped during a very dry summer. It was common sense.

The chickens were always good indicators of any potential movement, threatening or otherwise, because they investigated whatever moved. They didn't necessarily close in on the movement unless it was a fat beetle for instance, but they were alert and observant. You knew if something was around because they saw it. That summer the chickens were something like feathered alarms mostly owing to their body language, but unfortunately they were not everywhere at once. The Guineas hadn't arrived yet, but this summer was one reason that they joined the flock later on.

Around mid-July temperatures were around their highest points in the year, and mornings were the best times to take care of the vegetable garden, set water lines, pull weeds, and harvest vegetables. One morning, while we were in the garden, one of the two dogs, as there were the two by then, became intensely interested in something in a small comfrey patch behind the bay laurel tree. This particular dog was extremely good-natured, quiet, and had an air of wisdom about him. He was also always curious. He had been observed frolicking with a jackrabbit, each running around the other until both were tired, and then each going his or her separate way.

When he was intrigued by something in the comfrey patch, there was no cause for alarm, until there was a high pitched cry. He ran toward the back door of the house. My first thought was that a rattlesnake had bitten him, and sure enough, he had been bitten. He had to be taken to a veterinarian immediately. His friend, the Aussie, was brought into the house where he would be safe.

I didn't look down as I crossed the footbridge, until I reached its other side. Then I glanced down, saw, and heard the rattlesnake coiled at my feet with its head back and mouth open. There is no accounting for how I suddenly found myself on the back stoop, a good fifty feet away. The snake was undoubtedly as surprised as I was. I had the impression that it might have struck out, but it was impossible to know that.

It emerged from the comfrey patch a short while later, but neither it nor the comfrey patch survived the incident, even though both were a part of the natural world. Meanwhile our dog arrived at the clinic barely in time and thankfully survived the snake bite very well, but after that he was always wary about movement on the ground when he couldn't clearly see what it was that was moving.

Within a month of this incident, the second rattlesnake appeared. It was near the footbridge and was not happy, because it was buzzing loudly. At a moment like that you became instantly cautious, but at first glance there was no obvious rattlesnake. Then, there it was all right, next to the garden's chicken barrier, the bird netting that surrounded the garden. It didn't seem to move very much but it was not a happy rattlesnake.

It looked to be way too large a snake for comfort, and you couldn't immediately see that it was actually entangled in the netting and couldn't get away. Our dear friend and neighbor came over and noticed that it was caught in the netting. Immediately the rattlesnake didn't seem to be quite so large. The truth was that we knew of no way to free it and remain unbitten as we were not accustomed to handling snakes, and it wasn't a good idea to encourage a rattlesnake to take up residence by helping it to make itself comfortable. Its struggles had caused it to be seriously injured, and it was shot and buried. This snake was the only animal ever caught and injured in the bird netting surrounding the garden. Chickens of course eventually found places weakened by the hot summer sun and made their way through them to Nirvana within.

The third rattlesnake that summer arrived a few weeks later, and it was the grandfather of them all. It was in the garden, although it couldn't be clearly seen. It moved to the garden's edge and on through an opening in the netting, an opening with which the chickens were most likely familiar, so we were happy to find that and repair the netting.

By the time we were certain what caused the movement we had seen, the rattlesnake was already heading up the creek back to the hills. It moved quickly and with purpose. It might have been in the garden for a while, because the patterns on its latter half and most of its lower sides were a washed out bluish green that morphed to a grey brown on most of its back and toward its head. It was extremely thickset and perhaps a little more than five feet long. It apparently lived in the hills and probably came down the creek for a meal, where there was moisture and therefore prey.

We saw no obvious warning signs from any chicken that rattlesnakes were around, but it was also true that the chickens were nowhere near the rattlesnakes. No chicken that lived in the barn beside the creek was ever bitten by a rattlesnake.

Chickens seemed to know when to keep a respectful distance from whatever was causing the movement they almost certainly had spotted. They were quietly curious when it appeared they were uncertain of their own safety. Otherwise they generally clucked loudly, and of course Sarge shrieked, whenever anybody spotted walking, crawling, or running food.

Lush vegetation and mottled shadows on the ground in the garden were perfect camouflage for a rattlesnake.

The Skunk Feast

Meanwhile, the Silkies hatched and raised families of their own. There were several more soft, downy Silkies in their small enclosed area within the chicken house. By this time there were two reddish Silkies and one grey Silky, but all of them had gentle, friendly natures, all had soft feathers, and all had the usual feathered feet and bluish or bluish-tinted skin. They seemed placid and content, wandering about their home and yard, enclosed within the larger chickenyard, in the world and yet not of it.

One night something completely hideous happened. At first exactly what happened was unknown, although it was clear that predators were at work. When the chickenyard and chickenhouse doors were opened in the morning, no Silkies were to be seen moving around anywhere, although it was already daylight. There was no sound from the Silkies' ledge or under the ledge.

The Silkies were gone. They had just vanished. The door into their home was inside the chickenhouse, so it almost appeared as though someone must have made off with the sleeping Silkies, although who would do that, and why, was a complete mystery. People don't normally steal chickens, and anyway these were not show quality Silkies. They were backyard friends.

On closer inspection, in two places we saw where wire had been torn away from the wall for access into the Silkies' home. That wire had been solidly attached, and it looked as though something using a fair amount of force had grasped the wire and ripped it back. But where were the Silkies?

Most of the morning was spent searching for clues to the whereabouts of the Silkies. Finally one, just one, small white Silky feather was found behind the barn near its back door, in a little area of disturbed earth where there was a small depression. The depression was just at the base of the barn siding, and it left a very small opening leading to the space under the floorboards of the barn. There wasn't much space on the creek side of the barn, because the barn was leaning in that direction. On the older orchard side, flooring was still a few feet off the ground, and there was considerable space beneath the floorboards.

Now it was tragically obvious that something had successfully made off with the Silkies, and that this something had killed them. A raccoon or a skunk seemed the most likely culprit, but the ground around the depression was hard. There were no tracks to be seen, and no fur was caught on barn wood anywhere around. It was baffling.

This was horrible beyond words. It felt as though their house and yard that had seemed to be so safe for them had also resulted in their entrapment. It felt just like murder. In a way it was nature at work, since predation is nothing if not a part of the natural world. We have encroached into formerly undeveloped habitat, forcing other dwellers to live with us and around us. Naturally opportunism exists.

There was a small depression in the ground, just to the left of the barn's back door. A lone white, clean, fluffy Silky feather was found there.

This still pierced us because we felt as though we had failed in our responsibility to successfully care for the Silkies. We had twisted circumstance and opportunity. We had been outwitted, and the cost was very dear.

The Silkies' house and yard were dismantled, and never again were there Silkies living within that chickenhouse. Placing any more Silkies at risk was not an option. They were lovely little creatures and were not especially resilient, combative, or confrontational when provoked or in danger, like the Rhode Island Reds were when they had to be. Although the Silkies had probably done whatever they were capable of doing, they were no match for a strong predator with healthy canines, and they had almost surely been asleep. They were small, gentle, and delicate.

But the show wasn't over. The second half of it happened near the door at the front of the barn. While the back door was located near the creek, the front door was on the other side, near the older orchard that lined the driveway. There was plenty of space under the barn near this door. A ramp led up to the door, and beneath the ramp there were a couple of feet of barn siding from floor to ground. Beneath the ramp was a good place for a concealed opening into the dark, hidden space under the barn, because the ramp blocked your line of sight.

A few nights later, when we happened to look out from the sliding glass doors in the back room toward the front of the barn, we spotted movement beneath that ramp.

The night was dark, but the security light was on. It was positioned fairly high on the trunk of a tall walnut tree close to the garage, a little toward the house. It didn't interfere with the driveway. The lower limbs of this tree had been pruned away so the only limbs left were quite high up the tree trunk, and the tree was already old. No limbs interfered with anything, the garage, the driveway, or any thing else. Light flooded out from the bare but somewhat gnarled trunk of the tree and spread over the entire driveway, the front of the barn, the back of the house, part way into the older orchard and most of the way toward the creek.

There actually was movement just beneath that barn ramp, but within its shadow. Then, one by one, four half grown skunks emerged into the open. They wandered here and there, apparently enjoying being outside. At least two or three adult skunks followed the small ones. The number of skunks was almost unbelievable, only there they were, in living black and white. There was no way to know when they had arrived or how long they had been living there, and that was unsettling.

Just beneath the ramp to the barn's front door was a space hidden from view, when you looked at the barn straight on. It was hidden by the ramp, which was fairly steep.

We lost count because we were so intently watching the scene that was unfolding right before our eyes. The young skunks were playing with one another. They were running, stalking each other, batting at one another, jumping at each other and playing tag, like kittens do. They were having a marvelous time. The adults were wandering about but seemed more or less to be watching the younger ones at play. Meanwhile, still a few more adult skunks emerged from under the barn.

This felt like sneakily watching life's personal moments that we weren't supposed to see, but we did it anyway. It was fascinating, and there were no signs that playtime would stop any time soon. A couple of adults wandered toward the creek and darkness, but the chickens were carefully locked away for the night, and chicken wire was double and triple-checked shortly after the Silkies went missing. Any places that

There was open space from the barn on to the back of the house where the glass doors were. Skunks were everywhere. The adults headed toward the creek to the right of the barn, where light faded and then disappeared.

appeared even remotely vulnerable were strengthened as much as possible, short of constructing jail bars for them all.

A very large, old walnut tree grew a short distance away, behind the garage, in front of the barn and near the creek. It was a spectacular old tree, unencumbered by other trees, with a full, rounded crown that managed to block out most of the illumination from the security light. Otherwise there would have been more light in the area right next to the creek. We could still see the chickenyard door, but as adult skunks moved closer to the creek, they disappeared into darkness.

The little skunks, still playing, began as a group to slowly edge toward darkness near the creek, not far from the chickenyard. We wanted photos before they all left, and we also wanted to know that more chickens weren't in danger. We went out the back door onto the back stoop. This was on the other side of the house, and it wasn't brightly lit like the yard in front of the barn was. It seemed dark and safe. We edged from that corner of the house into the breezeway and toward the open area. We could just peer around the corner of the garage and see the frolicking skunks.

They were still there, and they instantly spotted us. They started to run helter-skelter, some into the older orchard, some in the opposite direction toward the creek, and some around the back of the garage into the darkness of the back yard, in the direction of the back stoop. What an unexpected and dreadful turn of events. The back door on that stoop was our only unlocked entrance into the house, and there was a slew of very upset and frightened skunks on all sides. Finally, after what seemed like a very long time of not moving and staying deathly quiet, we inched our way toward

96

the back stoop. No skunks were in sight, and we hurried inside.

The chickens were safe for another night, we weren't sprayed, and the skunks apparently didn't go back under the barn. We didn't take photos.

Later on, we wondered whether an extended skunk family had been making its way down the creek toward the marshlands for the hot summer months, and along the way had opportunistically grabbed the Silkies because there were so many mouths to feed. It was the time of year when those migrations often occurred. At least, it explained why the skunks didn't head very far into the orchard or up the creek after they were startled, but instead ran toward the creek and then headed south down the side of the creek, with some of them finding themselves in the back yard. From the crashing sounds they were making, it seemed that those that ran into the orchard on the far side of the creek actually backtracked and then followed the creek bed toward the road and summer quarters.

What really happened remained a mystery. Anything else was pure speculation, except that skunks are hungry, they play, they're clever, they're strong, and they successfully made off with our Silkies. We felt like murderers for a long time afterward.

The Neighborhood Dogs

The chickens were in danger from more than wildlife. They had to watch for domesticated life as well. The aforementioned neighbor's dog was around the area for quite a long time. Occasionally you'd see it running around the orchard, apparently enjoying itself, but when it approached the barn and the chickenhouse, it preferred a quiet and furtive approach. Its manner and body language revealed underlying aggression.

If it was close by and saw you, and you saw it, it exhibited what seemed to be a shifty demeanor. It stood up straight, tail stiff, but kept its head low and nose outstretched, maybe sniffing the air for chickens. When it was on its home turf it was quite friendly. When it was around the barn, where, incidentally, it knew that it was not supposed to be, it always kept several feet between itself and anyone who might try to grab it or head it away from the chickens.

One day it arrived uninvited at the back yard and headed toward the creek and footbridge where we were at the time. The chickens were out and about, happily scratching around in the ditch near their chickenyard and as it happened, also making their way toward the garden. Although they spotted the unpleasant dog, we were close by and that seemed to help somehow, because they normally ran to their chickenhouse. The unpleasant dog was quiet and watchful, but I managed to pet it and grab its collar, and then began to lead it to the other side of the barn and into the orchard on that side. Across that orchard was the house where it should have stayed.

At first I thought it was considering biting. Even though it knew me from friendly meetings elsewhere, it was surly and its ears were back. It really didn't want to leave the area where the chickens were, and it didn't like being led away. Finally it moved along, and when we were far enough away from the barn and closer to its home, I released it, clapping hands and telling it loudly to "Go Home." It didn't want to go. I glared at it and blocked it from returning. Then someone at its home began to call. Eventually, it went away.

Its owner came over to see whether any more chickens were dead, but fortunately none were. Then he insisted that his dog would never hurt a chicken. Unfortunately we had already seen what this dog was capable of doing, and so had he. So began a time of a strained friendship with this individual, creating a difficult situation all around. It felt like you were fighting a losing battle between what was witnessed but cast aside, and what was a fantasy world in which there was no recourse for finding solutions.

In any event, this dog either did not or was not allowed to wander our way again. Maybe there was concern for its safety. Certainly there was major concern for the chickens' safety. A little time passed but then not long after the dog had been escorted away from the chickens, we were asked if we had seen it. Apparently it had disappeared. At our house there had been occasional discussions about what might happen if we caught this dog killing more chickens, but we honestly hadn't seen it and didn't know where it was.

What do you say to an owner who truly loves his dog but who has not kept it within the safety of certain boundaries? We had seen it near young calves perhaps a quarter of a mile away, far behind the barn and through the orchards, in a small valley and field nestled at the base of the hills. We already knew that the rancher to whom these cattle belonged was prone to shooting dogs chasing his cattle, and asking questions later. And there were equally well-protected sheep in larger acreages not far away.

We said nothing about calves or sheep. The dog was apparently gone, and we did feel a little guilty for the hurt that its owner was obviously experiencing. That didn't mean that we missed the dog. There was no doubt in anybody's mind that the chickens didn't miss it either.

Nearly all the other dogs that were seen in our area were passing through and continued on their way. At one point a loosely knit pack of dogs living in the nearby town visited the area. During the night they explored the neighborhood, sometimes causing problems with livestock. Most were people's quiet pets during the day. This group was seen in our neighborhood only a few times during summer months one year, walking along a path far away in the orchard behind the barn. We didn't see them come any closer, good news because they didn't seem to realize there were chickens not too far away, or else they didn't care.

Our own dogs enjoyed watching the chickens. They didn't harm them, although the first puppy kept trying to herd them when he matured. The chickens didn't understand why he wanted them in a group, and they merely shuffled about here and there, much to his frustration. They were tending to the serious business of foraging and were unwilling to remain bunched together, unable to scratch or find bugs as easily as they liked to do. He tried to keep them in a small group, but eventually he gave up, to a point. Then he regularly checked in at the chickenyard, looking around to see where they all were. His presence around the chickens was like ours was. We were all basically outsiders in their realm.

The Mallard Pair

In early spring, creek waters occasionally ran high and then receded when rainstorms abated, but running surface water often remained until late spring or early summer. The exact time that the creek went dry depended upon rainfall during the winter months, with runoff and the level of the aquifer. Even when there wasn't much depth to the water in most of the creek, there were places where heavy winter currents had scoured away parts of creek banks, eventually forming quiet pools with gentle currents.

The creek ran through privately owned land. Activity that occurred around it was mostly confined to landowners out walking in their orchards, tractors passing it when orchards were being tilled, wildlife wandering around it and through it, and chickens foraging in it and on its banks. As it curved past hillsides, through orchards, and along the side of the barn and house, the land bordering it was peaceful and undisturbed.

In early spring fresh, green grass blanketed its sides, native wildflowers bloomed, and non-natives thrived too. Velvet green and brown mosses of various shapes and sizes, short and spongy, or with

Like the chickens, our dogs enjoyed fields and creek.

Loki liked to follow the basketball through the culvert and down the creek, while Bo preferred to try catching it.

long clumps of thread-like filaments, grew close to the water's edges and grew submerged along the creek bottom. Insects hovered over the surface and skeeters darted through gentle ripples. Dragonflies, damselflies, and butterflies flashed here and there. This incredible habitat attracted and generated life. Many different species of birds migrated through the general area on their way north, and some remained to raise young before the hot summer arrived. The nearby lake was

home to numerous species of waterfowl, of whom many were permanent residents.

Every year a pair of mallards flew over the orchard, coming from the direction of the lake and heading up the little creek. They arrived without fail. They rested in areas where water was gently moving in wide pools. If winter rains had been generous, there were more of these areas, and they found wider swaths of water close to the barn and the house. If not, they found secret pools further upstream, closer to the hills.

This pair circled the area they'd chosen in any given spring, landed, settled down, and swam contentedly in the little pool they'd chosen for nesting. They generally flew back and forth, from lake to creek and back, several times over a period of a few weeks, before you didn't see them in the air any more. Then you knew that they were going about the business of hatching out and raising their brood of ducklings.

If you walked too close to the creek without noticing them, they remained very quiet until you were nearly upon them, and suddenly you were all equally startled at seeing one another. They flew upward and circled, returning when you'd gone on your way. A few times the dogs chanced upon them and tried sniffing them, and of course they took flight, squawking as they rose, but they came back as soon as they knew the dogs had passed by. No one ever tried to harm them.

One year this pair chose a pool that was not far above the chickenyard and culvert. A nice, wide swath of the creek gave rise to a comfortably deep pool, forming a graceful curve around an extremely old plum tree planted by an ancestor. This tree, the grassy creek banks, and the creek were beautiful in early spring when the tree was in full bloom, its white blossoms blanketing its branches, floating upon the water's gently moving surface, and falling into the newly green grasses. Around this time of the year, the mallard pair arrived and completed a picture of perfect tranquility.

They were quiet nearly all of the time but when disturbed or for other reasons not generally understood, they quacked loudly. That year they were more vocal than usual, because the chickens foraged along the creek banks and often startled them. After a while they seemed to grow accustomed to red combs appearing around the corner of the grassy banks and softly cooing hens wandering in search of food.

As usual the chickens were engrossed in their own activities and didn't pay much, if any, attention to the mallard pair. It was the mallard pair that reacted at first. They seemed to find themselves living around and within the world of chickens, but that was about the extent of it. Chickens serenely foraged close by, while the mallards watched them.

We rarely saw ducklings making their way downstream with their parents, but they delighted us when we did see them. Perhaps the little family was careful to travel the distance to the lake in a silent and unobtrusive manner. They undoubtedly moved from their little creek home as soon as they were able, probably soon after the ducklings hatched, because there were too many predators along that little channel.

You had to catch the timing of the move just right in order to see them leave. Most of the time, we noticed that they had moved on only because the parents didn't quack or startle, taking off and circling their little home. One day the family was simply gone.

The Huge Gopher Snake

There were reptiles other than rattlesnakes in the neighborhood. A few species of lizards were plentiful, and occasionally a blue and black striped garter snake made its way into the yard or the garden. Gopher snakes were around, as well as king snakes. Most were small and were probably not very old. Most went peacefully on their way without incident and thankfully without finding themselves in any danger.

By and large the chickens left lizards and snakes alone, although they had been conspicuously absent from the garden and its vicinity during those times when rattlesnakes were around. The chickens didn't seem to mind if lizards and other snakes were close by. They didn't seem to care one way or another. At times they scratched and ate very close to a gopher or garter snake, but as usual they were engrossed in their own daily existence, and a harmless snake or two really wasn't a part of their very important daily routine.

One day the king of all gopher snakes appeared. This happened near the creek bank, upstream of the chickenhouse, on the far side of the creek. It was around late summer, the day was hot, and no grass was growing in the orchard. What had grown along the sides of the creek was mostly dried, having matured and gone to seed. The only moisture in the soil was probably a foot below the surface, so the soil surface itself was hard and dry. The hot noonday sun overhead leached away the vibrancy of colors of orchard and earth.

We were in the orchard with the dogs and were coming back toward the barn when we heard it. It was a breathy, raspy, hissing sound that was loud enough to carry across several rows of trees. It wasn't a buzzing rattle, and that was good news, but the sound was loud, and you couldn't miss that something was very upset.

When we gazed toward the creek we could see its silhouette. It was a snake, it was coiled, and it was simply enormous. Both dogs had run toward it and were standing near it, staring curiously at it, not moving, and that disturbed it even more. It stared back and hissed. Its extremely large head could easily be seen, because although the snake was on the same side of the creek as we were, its profile formed a perfect silhouette against the far creek bank. Its head and part of its body were at the same height as Bo's face and Loki's chest. The dogs hadn't moved, so it was easy to see how large this snake actually was. Its colors weren't quickly discernible at that distance because they were washed out by the hot summer sun, but we could see that it had patterns of color, and that they were most likely shades of gray and brown.

The atmosphere was electric, and we were terrified. We couldn't determine exactly what kind of snake this was, from several rows of trees away. We figured that the dogs' lives were probably at stake, and thankfully they did come away when they were called. That is, Loki came and Bo, who was deaf from birth, obeyed hand signals and followed him. There were no strikes and no cries of pain. With a huge sigh of relief and the dogs safely restrained beside us, we carefully walked closer to the snake, watchful that the dogs stayed well away from it.

The snake didn't move at all, and we thought this was strange. It lay there staring at us, hissing with harsh breath, but it made no effort to leave. Finally, when we were a bit closer to it, we could see that it was a gopher snake, with its head still in silhouette and with recognizable patterns on its body. The question was why it remained so aggressive and, well, why it remained. Perhaps all gigantic snakes felt comfortable enough to hold their ground, but normally a snake would leave, wanting nothing to do with us.

Finally we were close enough to understand. Even though it was an enormous and intimidating snake, and that was more than enough to keep us at a distance, it had stayed because it had been hunting, and it had been successful. It was coiled upon a mound of soft, moist earth, in fact a large, freshly made gopher mound, and the unlucky occupant had not escaped. The snake grasped its meal in its mouth and was clearly reluctant to lose that meal to a lowly dog. It held its ground tenaciously.

It must have been at least three inches in diameter or maybe a little more, and there was no way to tell how long it was. Because it was coiled upon itself, its main bulk was off the ground. That bulk was resting on top of the gopher mound, and this was the reason the snake was so well profiled when we were some distance away.

Somehow it seemed rude and less than comfortable to

Further up the creek was good habitat for an enormous gopher snake.

stay and intrude on the snake's meal, so we breathed a sigh of relief and left, since our presence had already upset the snake enough. The only nagging thought was that the snake was not very far up the creekbed from the chickenhouse. The gopher mound upon which it was coiled was only as far away as just past the plum tree.

The chickens would probably cheerfully make their way along the creek banks, eating and chuckling among themselves, noticing the snake but possibly ignoring it, even though it looked large enough to open its jaws and comfortably swallow a chicken. On the other hand, they deserved more faith from us. They had shown us time and again that they were more aware of potential danger than we were.

The huge snake was never seen again. Maybe it was on its way along the creek bed to the hills, after heading downstream for food and water. Perhaps it was not interested in rodents closer to the barn. Possibly it saw the chickens and left. Probably it digested its meal and preferred not to be around curious dogs and scratching chickens, whose feet ended in very large claws. It probably preferred the peace and quiet of the hills nearby and left civilization, intrusive dogs, wary but interested humans, and scratching chickens behind.

What might have happened if chickens met snake remained a mystery. Perhaps the chickens did meet the snake, or maybe the snake met the chickens. We heard no shrill shrieks from Sarge and saw no chicken or chickens in attack mode, flapping their wings at something or fiercely scratching at something with their giant, three toed, clawed feet.

The chickens had already taught us that they had their own innate store of knowledge and their own secretive ways, and we knew they would have done whatever they thought was necessary for their own safety.

The protective measures we had taken to keep the Silkies safe had backfired in an ugly way. Life is full of insufficient knowledge and unexpected events, and you can't always assume that your thoughts, assumptions or plans are infallible. Thankfully, this time, no chickens disappeared.

The Coyotes

Coyotes often frequented the neighborhood and were likely to appear around seasonal changes during the year, or at least it seemed that way. They could be heard calling to one another when there was some distance between one or more of them, or howling and chuckling among themselves when they were in a group. In the fall and late fall, they were around more often and on occasion came fairly close to the house and the barn. They called as they traveled up and down the hills, and you could see them running across the cattle and hay fields nestled against the hills.

Their howls were heard most often at dusk or after dark, coming from the direction of the hills behind the barn. At night they also traveled along the paths and dirt roads that went through the orchards. You found tracks and scat there, and you knew they'd passed through. Usually they traveled across the hills and around the edges of the neighborhood on their way somewhere, and then after a few days, they appeared to follow the same route back, or at least their howls and cries went one way and then came back that same way. Although they were only occasionally seen and more often heard, exactly where, when, and how far they roamed was their secret.

They usually stayed some distance away from the barn when they traveled at night. Although we thought about coyotes grabbing a fat hen for their dinner, we didn't worry too much about it since the chickens were safely locked in the barn whenever the coyotes were anywhere in the neighborhood. Or so we thought. Maybe it was true, but on the other hand, a coyote that wanted a chicken wouldn't be inclined to play its hand in front of us.

The chickens never suffered from a raid by hungry coyotes, but that didn't mean that we knew everything that was going on in the natural world, even in our back yard. It seemed that only someone who was unaware would assume that he or she knew all the movements and strategies of a coyote, or a skunk, or a raccoon, or for that matter, of a chicken. Most definitely of a chicken.

One evening well after dark, Bo, the deaf Australian shepherd, wanted to run out into the orchard before settling down for the night. His friend Loki generally looked after him, but Loki preferred to stay in. Because there were no moon and very few stars, the night was dark. Bo couldn't see hand signals and was on a long lead line. We were enjoying the evening air and were walking a good distance away from the house, well beyond the soft glow cast by the yard security light.

All at once coyotes began to howl, and it sounded like there were quite a few of them. They were calling and howling as a group, and it sounded like they were walking along a road that ran through an orchard next to us, fairly close by. They were far enough away for their conversations to be a little muted. Then, the howls and cries became louder, and then louder, and still louder. They were coming straight toward us and were making a great deal of noise. What they wanted was uncertain, but knowing they were headed right at us was unsettling, and we didn't wait to find out what they wanted, if anything. By now the very loud howls unhinged any sense of comfort we'd had in the dark orchard. I reeled in the dog who was aware of the coyotes, although I knew that he couldn't hear them.

We headed back to the house, and the coyotes followed us even more closely. We didn't know why, and hazarding a guess when we were still in the dark and not very close to the house was a bad idea. Finally we emerged from the darkness into the glow of the security light, and made it to the back stoop and the back door of the house.

We had never known them to come so close to the house, and by now they were actually between the house and the barn, very close to the chickens. They obviously knew where we were and must have known the chickens were nearby, but they didn't seem to be interested in chickens, which was a disconcerting thought. After a short time they headed back into the orchard. Their conversations faded as they went on their way toward the hills, continuing on to wherever they were headed.

Once safely inside the house, we figured that this was an interesting event. It was almost as though the coyotes were out for an evening stroll, curiosity got the better of them, and they followed us home. There wasn't really a sense of danger except from what was probably an overactive imagination, although maybe if opportunity in the form of a healthy, plump dog presented itself, and there were enough of them, they might have taken advantage. Fortunately they didn't come that close to the house and barn again, although we wouldn't have known if they had unless they were deep in conversation at the time.

The Oblivious Chickens

It wasn't true that the chickens were unconcerned with the various fauna that lived around them and sometimes within their territory. The chickens knew who was there. Of course they knew. They simply had their ways. They lived within their society, and they were complete. They didn't need anyone else. If a garter snake made its way past them, it was all right. If a group of birds flew over their heads and landed in a tree a few feet from them, they didn't mind. If they felt threatened, they reacted to keep themselves safe, Sarge shrieking and whistling and the hens running, wings flapping madly to help them back to the safety of the chickenyard, as fast as their round, rolling bodies could carry them. When they were running to safety they were surprisingly fast.

They foraged contentedly as birds winged past them, snakes crawled by, squirrels scolded overhead, fish migrated upstream, and lizards ran past their large tripod feet. Multitudes of animals of all sizes lived in the same area as the chickens, but as long as there were no threats, everybody lived peacefully in close proximity to one another.

On the other hand, when there actually was a threat from another animal, like a hawk or the neighbor's unfriendly dog, the chickens took action to remove themselves from harm's way. They never, ever remained complacent, although how they knew when to act was often a mystery, for instance, when water was very close to covering the footbridge that they used, or when the snake slithering past them was not a rattlesnake or more to the point, was a rattlesnake, and it was time to edge away and clear the area.

The chickens were well aware of what was going on within their own personal neighborhood, but they lived their own lives, allowing other creatures to live theirs.

Chapter 7

The Flock Lives On

Sarge Ages
New Roosters
Son of Sarge
Assisted Living for Sarge
Requiem for Sarge

There is little that is as upsetting as the realization that a dear friend and companion is nearing the end of his life on this earth, a friend who has been faithful to his own nature and way of being and has created no harm to anyone else, and that is completely remarkable in itself. Perhaps it is apprehension of the unknown that you face. What you knew through the years as an integral part of your own life is also nearing its end.

Sarge possessed charm and radiated class, for a chicken. We selfishly wanted him to go on forever, but that was not possible. He was handling the inevitable with aplomb, but like all selfish beings, we were not.

Sarge Ages

The natural passage of time took its toll on Sarge, and by the time he was six, going on seven, his appearance revealed his age. He was still a magnificent rooster, but his movements were slightly less graceful and more stiff then they had been. His wattles were very long and still bright red, although there was a touch of a deeper hue, and his comb showed scars and folding here and there. It still stood straight up and was large and impressive, but it appeared older and at times a bit pale or a bit dark, hinting that his heart was physically no longer as strong as it had been. After all, he'd lived a lifetime of caring for his flock, he'd always had a wonderful heart, and he had used it to its fullest throughout his entire life.

His long, sturdy legs and feet were still long and sturdy but a little more knobby, and they appeared swollen here and there. His spurs and claws had to be trimmed more often because he wasn't as active, and they didn't wear down on their own any more. He had always worn down his claws himself but as he aged, he moved more slowly and covered less distance. Actually his spurs were trimmed periodically anyway because Sarge was not a chicken that sought battle. He was a protector and a leader. He didn't require spurs that grew so long that they interfered with his movements.

His feathers were still rust red and shiny, and his tail feathers were still blue black, glistening in the sunlight and falling in a rippling cascade of deep and intense color, but they seemed less vibrant somehow. It was like seeing a bright red apple in spring sunlight and then seeing it again in late summer at dusk. It was still bright red in essence but its physical environment had changed. Sarge's physical self, the self that gave form to who he was, was changing.

He was active in leading the flock to forage, and he shrieked and whistled when he found food or spotted what might be danger, but he had lost the impetus of his youth. He appeared to be less impatient and less compelling, although he was still a fine figure of a rooster. Sarge aged gracefully.

It was painful for everyone to see these changes that were taking place, even though this was after all a part of life. Sarge was still active, but it was increasingly obvious that he was not really able to get around very well. It was plain that he had aches and pains that truly affected him, at times severely. The time for his retirement was rapidly approaching. No one wanted to contemplate anything beyond that time, or what retirement for Sarge really meant. He was completely treasured.

New Roosters

The best solution was that Sarge should live on in spirit, since his body was aging and he didn't have very much time left. As a result of that decision, Sarge's progeny were hatched out and raised. They were observed from the time they were chicks until they were nearly past adolescence, with Sarge's special traits kept in mind. Hopefully the rooster chosen to eventually become head of the flock would exhibit at least some of those very special characteristics that made Sarge such a special chicken. Continuity and peace in the chickenhouse and chickenyard would prevail.

Leadership, courage in the face of danger, desire to find food and to not eat it all, an ability to live and let live with regard to the presence of beings other than chickens, including humans, a certain savoir faire, and many other ideals would be wonderful traits for the future Sarge Junior to have. Sarge had them all and then some. Sarge's children were carefully watched in case they exhibited some of these exceptional attributes. A medium sized rooster would be perfect, just like Sarge.

As the adolescents matured and became old enough, they were placed in the chickenhouse and chickenyard with the adult chickens. That way, they interacted

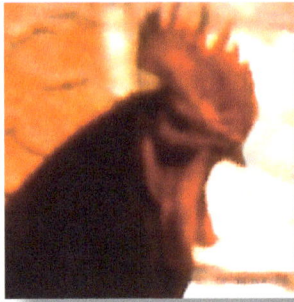

with the flock. Hopefully one would stand out from the rest and be the best chicken to carry the flock forward into the future. There was hopeful anticipation for the flock to continue onward in an atmosphere of happy clucking and cooing, governed and protected by Sarge Junior.

One by one, the young roosters were weeded out for less than exceptional behavior, for weakness, for being too large, for being too small, or for some other reason that set them too far apart from Sarge. Eventually one remained and was left to mature with the young hens hatched at the same time as the baby roosters. It seemed likely that over time, he would ease into a position of responsibility, and Sarge would fade, because of his rapidly advancing old age and rapidly increasing inability to get around very well. We figured that timing was important and thought that we had come close to managing it fairly well. We still had so much to learn about chickens.

Son of Sarge

The young rooster settled into the flock's routine and was absorbed into it as a bona fide member, just like his sisters. The young chickens still kept to themselves in a group much of the time, but gradually they edged away from the safety of their small social circle and became true flock members, although they were at the lower end of the pecking order. The young rooster behaved much as the hens did.

Then they matured to a point at which the young hens began to lay eggs. That meant the young rooster was also a young adult. For a while he wandered along with the rest of the group, and Sarge was still the leader, although he didn't travel very far any more. By this time, Sarge had difficulty walking and stayed close to the chickenhouse the vast majority of the time. All seemed to be progressing according to the plan, or so we thought.

One day, in the late morning, there was a fuss in the back yard. There were cries and there were screeches, and they sounded vaguely like chickens. Then we saw Sarge sprinting toward the patio where he was chased into a corner by, of all things, his son. This was an absolutely horrible and despicable turn of events. Sarge was wounded, bleeding from his comb. We rescued him at once and chased the now incredibly ugly young rooster back toward the chickenhouse.

First of all it was important to gently care for Sarge, to calm him and reassure him, and to wash and dress his wounds. They weren't severe at all. It turned out that there were only a few light scratches on his comb, but they needed to be cleaned and a soothing antibiotic salve applied. By far the most hideous wound that Sarge had suffered was to his pride and his reason for living. He really was too old to care for the flock, had been even more rapidly failing, and clearly had very little time left. The flock needed a rooster, and Sarge needed peace.

We hadn't realized how awful introducing another rooster would be for him, mostly because we didn't think that another rooster, if chosen carefully, would challenge an aging and decrepit Sarge. We had seen other roosters living together, and while they were wary of each other, the elderly rooster that was not even around the hens that much was not normally challenged that we could see, at least not in an ugly physical fight, and especially not when there was plenty of space for both to coexist. We had noticed that the role of head chicken seemed to pass from one rooster to another when the first became unable to get around. Of course in the natural world, males fight over females and battles can be to the death. We simply hadn't witnessed that in chickens. There seemed to be a civilized way in which the torch was passed. We obviously didn't understand or take into account the minutiae of behavioral innuendo involved, and we clearly didn't appreciate the individual nature of each and every chicken.

The awful truth was that the immature rooster had a personality that sort of flipped when he matured, and he became mean. He became known as Son of Sarge. Literally overnight, after he chased and injured Sarge, he became a vicious despot toward the hens, and he hunted us whenever we were around. Much to our dismay he sprouted upward, and in no time at all he became unpleasantly huge. But he had remained mild until that fateful day. Then he became a terror, and this change happened so quickly we were in a state of shock.

Meanwhile, Sarge needed care, and he needed to be kept safe, even though he wanted with all his heart to return to the chickenyard. He protested but moved into the garage where his wounds were watched, cleansed, and treated, so they didn't become infected. Like any chicken he enjoyed dusting himself in the dirt, and that wasn't possible until his wounds were healed.

For a few days this worked, but a decision was in the offing. Then late one morning the decision was made for us. The flock, including Son of Sarge, was foraging just across the creek from the chickenhouse. On the opposite side of the creek about thirty feet away from them all, I was walking toward the house. Suddenly I felt a tremendous force hit my back from behind, so hard it knocked me over. When my back was turned, Son of Sarge had launched himself at me and had knocked me down.

This was an evil chicken. We thought that only a coward attacks you from behind, although in truth it is probably a good battle maneuver. The point was that Sarge would never have gone into battle against us, and for many years we had lived without problems alongside him and his flock. Son of Sarge was still young, and it was disturbing to contemplate how seriously aggressive he might eventually become.

That very hour, Son of Sarge met his end behind the barn. He dressed out at

The hostile Son of Sarge took off from the lower left corner, near the creek, and attacked in flight in the upper right corner, near the back of the garage.

about eight pounds, traveled south in a freezer, and became chicken and dumplings that had to be thrown out because the chicken part was too tough.

This had been a very hard lesson. No one would ever have wanted to hurt Sarge or to allow him to be hurt, not in any way. He was an amazing being. The knowledge that he had been hurt because of our ignorance caused intense guilt and a truly awful feeling in our hearts. Thereafter, whenever it became necessary to introduce a younger rooster, first the older rooster lived out his life and passed peacefully away. The new rooster was chosen primarily for his mild personality, but he also had to be of medium size.

Assisted Living for Sarge

After Sarge's wounds had been cleaned, it was easy to see that they were few and that they were really quite minor. Unfortunately, aside from his wounds, when we carefully observed him Sarge was just too old and in too much pain, possibly from arthritis and more, to return to the chickenhouse. He was nearly unable to jump up onto the bench to roost and to jump down again in the morning. He was slightly shaky and stiff, and could easily have fallen and hurt himself even more. So he remained in the back yard, where he relaxed and stretched his wings out over the grass in the sunshine. Hens visited him. He seemed content. All of us, including the dogs, spent time with him so he wasn't alone. A large round from the trunk from the bay laurel made a nice chair at its base, and it was pleasant, and decent, to take work there and sit near him. He slept in the garage where he was safe.

In the morning, he was lifted from his sleeping area on the shop bench, part of which was covered with fresh newspaper changed daily, and where there were containers of food and water. During the day the containers were placed on the floor, just inside the small, open door nearest the house. He was carried to the sunshine on the sidewalk along the back yard, or if the grass was warm enough, on the back lawn. He seemed to be able to move more easily only after he rested in sunshine for about an hour. He lolled about on the grass most of the day, occasionally hobbling to his food and water, and at the end of the day, he patiently waited to be lifted to the workbench for his dinner and for the night, when he was closed in for safety. His superficial wounds were healing.

This routine lasted only for a few days before it was clear that Sarge was already in the process of passing on, and had been, before the evil Son of Sarge had chased him. This made us even angrier with Son of Sarge. We were glad we were rid of this chicken that clearly had been without ethics and values and had been like a chicken sociopath, at least as much as we understood it, and felt it.

It was time to release Sarge, the magnificent rooster. He was certainly in pain, and allowing him to suffer was not an option. He was failing very, very quickly, in fact almost by the hour. When he was so unsteady on his feet that he fell while standing in the sunlight, we knew that we could not allow him to suffer any longer. It happened instantly for him, when his head was turned away, by means of a twenty-two. He was buried in a deep grave beneath the huge, ancient bay laurel tree in the back yard. After all, he had spent many hours foraging around it and sneaking past it to lead his hens to the flower beds beyond. It was appropriate, and he deserved to rest there.

Requiem for Sarge

Sarge had touched all of us deeply. He was a dignified chicken and a loyal guardian of his flock. He possessed a delightful nature that seemed to take life's obstacles in stride and to deal with them with an aplomb that could only come from a soul that had natural class. Unfortunately he was truly blind sided by his son's attack, more than anything else because he had lived a comfortable and cheerful existence with his hens, alongside us for nearly all of his life, and he was ill-prepared for such unprecedented aggression.

He was pleasant, and he ignored us. Of his many wonderful traits, these were two that we had always realized he possessed but didn't fully appreciate, until the uncommonly twisted Son of Sarge matured and took over for an extremely brief moment in time.

Sarge was the first rooster who lived within our midst and within whose territory we lived. We all happily coexisted. The horrid turn of events at the end of Sarge's lifetime highlighted the realization that we didn't know as much as we previously thought we knew about other life forms on this planet that we call home. In this case, it was about chickens. We were reminded of how much misfortune resulted from of our lack of knowledge. It was humbling. It also reinforced our respect for Sarge and his innate good nature, spending his very last days in our company and with our protection, and yet maintaining his dignity, style, and composure. The only consolation during those couple of days was that he seemed to enjoy relaxing in the sun and seemed to be in good spirits. His extremely rapid physical deterioration was easy to see, not necessarily because he was upset, although he was, but because he was very ill and fading fast.

This was the end of an era. Sarge was gone. The rooster that had taught us what it meant to be a responsible, courteous, yet devoted guardian of the flock was no more. It felt good that we had done what we could for him in his old age and had not allowed him to suffer, but it felt horrible that we had so misjudged Son of Sarge, and he had really hurt the venerable old rooster. During his lifetime, Sarge shared what it meant to be a pleasant and dignified living creature. No one would ever forget him. Sarge had his own poem:

Passing On

Charcoal grey ether, edges of prisms
Of crimson, ochre, and indigo,
Quickening waves, pain causes chasms
Of anguish, shorn senses, vertigo.
No solace, no reprieve, nor ego,
Just endless, inexplicable spasms.

Once there was color, radiant, resounding,
Electric kaleidoscope,
Opals, star sapphires, emeralds abounding
In opulence, glowing sunscope,
Warm laughter, and always hope,
Harmonious good will surrounding.

Passages, ravages, blotches of time
Engraved upon body and soul,
Subliminal payments, a steady decline,
Nothing is ever left whole.
Youth pays a tedious toll
For living, loving in life's pantomime.

Mindlessly engulfed by agony, ecstasy,
Two sides of death, the same coin.
Waiting, for what? Wishing it ceaselessly,
Yet still, more time to purloin,
A little afraid to adjourn,
At last, passing on rather easily.

To every thing there is a season,
and a time to every purpose under the heaven.
Ecclesiastes 3:1

Chapter 8

A New Home and Chickenhouse

A Sturdy Chickenhouse
The Peacocks
The Yellow-Golden Pheasant
The Kingsnake

Some time after the passing of Sarge, we found ourselves purchasing a new home. It wasn't actually new. It was really quite old, but it was new to us, and as chance would have it, this home and orchard were a part of the same neighborhood and weren't far away. Environment and landscape were basically the same. But there wasn't a chickenhouse or a chickenyard, so we had to build them both.

Meanwhile the chickens needed to be moved, because the old barn's collapse was imminent. It was slanting precariously, leaning outward visibly more every day, and the time had come to dismantle it before it fell full force and scattered itself.

Our friends and neighbors generously offered to house the flock while we built a new home and yard. It was during this time that these good and kind people were astonished to see members of the flock chase and catch mice. These friends forgot more about chickens than we could ever hope to know, but apparently there is always more to learn about chicken minds and chicken society.

The hens and the new, young rooster of the flock went to live for some weeks with these wonderful friends. They gave the flock its own area, and all the chickens settled in nicely. The flock was completely safe and well-fed with these friends, but true to form they also chased and caught mice that foolishly wandered their way. Meanwhile we built a new chickenhouse and chickenyard, making each as strong as we could.

A Sturdy Chickenhouse

The new chickenhouse was once again behind the garage, although this time, there was no barn. Instead there was a shed that extended off the back of the garage. It was old, well built and solid, when two by fours were really two inches by four inches. It had been used to store wood, but the wood was moved, and the shed was cleaned and organized for storing equipment like mowers, rakes and shovels. It was also a place to keep shavings and metal containers of food for chickens.

The new chickenhouse was built off the back of the shed and looked out toward the orchard, which bordered other orchards that continued on toward the hills, until you reached the cattle fields nestled at their base. These were the same hills that the little bear had known so well. We used heavy lumber from the old barn for construction, and when the chickenhouse and chickenyard were completed, they looked as though they had always been a part of the garage and shed. Lumber for the barn and for buildings at this new location was from the same era, rough-sawn and unfinished.

Inside the new chickenhouse, there was a large, flat ledge. Unlike the ledges in the old barn, this one had been boarded across the front so naturally there wasn't any space under it, but that wasn't a problem. Resting on the top of the front edge was a roost, consisting of a simple frame with long, narrow boards attached at each side, running across, through holes drilled through a center board. The roosting frame was attached to the back wall by hinges about a foot above the ledge, leaving the frame slightly slanted toward the front and able to be lifted up for cleaning. You stood at the front of the roosting framework and placed any convenient board under it, since it wasn't heavy. Then you could easily sweep away used shavings and spread out fresh, clean shavings. When you were done, you removed whatever held the roost and let it down. This turned out to be an easy, ingenious way to keep the roosting area clean, and it only took a few moments.

Chickens could easily and comfortably settle themselves here, because the roost was strong with its cross boards quite close together, designed to fit large, tripod feet with claws. Edges were sanded and softened for the comfort of sleeping chickens. The front of the ledge and roost were not far off the ground but just in case, a small bench sat in front for the convenience of elderly chickens with a touch of arthritis.

Directly opposite the roosting area were the nest boxes. They were lined up and braced against the opposite wall, and each nest box had its own tiny ledge out in front. The chickens easily reached the nest boxes, stood on the little ledges, hovered expectantly over the hen already in The Nest Box of the day, and waited for their window of opportunity. As usual they all chose to use a special few nest boxes at any one time.

Like the chickenhouse in the old barn, the floor was covered with soft pine shavings. A long feeder was fastened against the wall, tucked in under the nest boxes and off the floor. A smaller feeder with oyster shells for calcium was right next to it. A large waterer was just around the corner, near an outdoor faucet. We hoped the chickens would feel at home.

A small door just their size led to the chickenyard outside, while we went into their house through a door from inside the shed, just as the inner door of their old home had been open to the inside of the barn. We found a large, paned glass window and placed it in the outer wall. It had been confiscated from somewhere else and actually looked as though it belonged there. We figured it added a homey touch.

Any place that was open was covered with chicken wire, including the roof of the chickenyard. When we found evidence of predators in the shed, out came the chicken wire to cover areas that we'd missed and they'd found. They hadn't managed to reach the chickens, not yet, but we weren't taking any chances.

The new chickenyard was an easy, roomy rectangle off the back of the chickenhouse, wrapping around it and meeting the back wall of the shed. Halfway up, that wall was open, so in went chicken wire. Telephone poles grayed by weather and sawn to length made good corner posts for the chickenyard. Once those poles were dug into place, there was no budging them.

Long two by fours from the old barn, real two by fours, full measure, stretched between the telephone poles for framing. The outer door of the chickenyard was none other than the weathered, gray front door of the

Weathered wood has great beauty. This door had been the entrance to the old barn since the barn had been built, over 100 years ago. It was not only beautiful, it probably had countless memories of its own.

old barn. We braced it open during daylight hours, so the chickens roamed and foraged as usual, but like before, we latched it shut at night, whenever the chickens needed to be safely sheltered, or whenever the garden needed to be safely sheltered.

We wanted safety. No one had forgotten Silkies and skunks, even though we could only do the best that we could manage. We hoped for the best and fastened wire to framing as though we expected the worst.

The chickens seemed content and cozy in their new home. They settled in without any fuss or stress at all and continued to lay eggs. The rooster in charge of the flock at that time was a quiet sort, not aggressive, and had been assimilated into the flock while he was still immature, shoved into the lowest position on the pecking order. There he had remained until he was an adult rooster. He began to come into his own, although he was never very assertive. He was of medium size, darker than Sarge had been and without the panache exhibited by Sarge, but he was pleasant. After Son of Sarge, we were grateful.

But Sarge himself was not there, and everyone felt his absence. The truth was that Sarge had been a star, and we missed him. The flock was not the same without Sarge, although there were always some interesting characters around. Now and then in your lifetime you run across a few individuals who stand out in every way, and Sarge had been one of those, even though he was a chicken. Maybe his nature was too expansive and could never have fit into the smaller chickenhouse. Maybe he had lived in the large, old, two-storied barn because that was where he had belonged. Maybe he was the chicken-in-charge that had existed in that place and time.

Sadly there was no creek of any size nearby, but there was a small runoff creek just under a hundred feet away, and there were fruit trees beside this small creek. The inevitable vegetable garden was uncomfortably close to the chickenhouse, but the garden had to have that open, sunny space. Some situations are never win-win.

Although the walnut orchard directly behind the chickenhouse and chickenyard consisted of huge, very old trees, they didn't quite reach over the chickenyard to create a shady spot for the chickens. However there was an old apricot tree just next to the chickenyard. Not only did the tree provide shade, in midsummer it also had overripe apricots on branches that were difficult to reach when they grew out over the top of the chickenyard. They fell through the chicken wire and into the chickenyard, where they didn't last more than a brief moment.

There was no remarkable old barn, there was no creek with bear tracks, and there was only an occasional rat that made its way over from neighboring fields and levees. There were still raptors in the general area, there were skunks and raccoons, and there were snakes, although few if any were rattlesnakes. Generally there were the same fauna and flora that had been around the old barn a few orchards away. The creek and its rich assemblage of plants and animals were missing.

The chickens and the quiet, unassuming, new rooster relaxed comfortably into their new turf. They had lived very well in the old barn, centered themselves around the creek and its four seasons, thoroughly enjoyed the garden, ravaged the flower beds and lawn, and in general had lived life to the fullest, with self assurance and sometimes with gusto, but also with a gentle happiness. Now they took over their new space with that same sense of tranquility.

The Peacocks

A corner of the new chicken complex became a home for four Guineas. They had their own small house, and their covered yard was shaded with honeysuckle climbing

The chickens liked their new home, but true to form, they also liked to wander. However they didn't care for snow and stayed close by, muttering under their breaths.

all over one side. They liked the honeysuckle. As it poked through the chicken wire, they grazed it away. Like the chickens, their door was open during the day, and they wandered about with the chickens, through the orchard, in and around the garden in winter, and near the small seasonal creek.

The Guineas generally kept to themselves in a little group, but that group was absorbed as an entity into the flock at large. Everyone wandered along the irrigation line by the fruit trees at the edge of the walnut orchard, because the perennial grass that grew beneath the fruit trees was soft, moist, and refreshing, wonderful on a hot day. Bugs and worms lived there too.

Everyone was particularly fond of the microenvironment beneath one extremely old and extremely large Gravenstein apple tree. It had taken on the general shape of an umbrella with grassy feet. It was a wonderful tree under which you could relax and doze in cool, green grass on warm afternoons, after you had eaten your way there. After a nice, comfortable rest, you scratched and ate your way back, and just before dusk, you wandered into your own individual yard.

Occasionally the Guineas found themselves in the chickenyard rather than in their own yard. It was never a problem as they simply kept themselves to themselves as a group on the chickens' roost for the night. No one was ever left outside overnight. Everyone was safe inside a house and all outer doors were closed.

Boysenberries grew along the seasonal creek. Wild turkeys enjoyed standing on support framework and leaning over to pluck ripe berries for breakfast.

You wouldn't have assumed that other animals noticed or cared about the difference between Guineas and chickens. As it turned out, two visiting peacocks did notice, and they did care. Still, Guineas were Guineas. They weren't peacocks. After the peacocks arrived one night, we were surprised when they appeared to be attracted to the Guineas. Probably the Guineas were even more surprised.

It all started in the middle of one black night, when all of us were jolted awake by a hair raising bellow. It sounded like whatever was making this noise was only a few feet away. It kept on and on, and on, and then there were two of whatever was bellowing. The air was electric with fascination, horror, some fear and ample dread. The sound was vaguely like a very loud donkey that is in excruciating pain.

There was nothing for it. We had to find the source, although it was clear that the only way to do it was very carefully. Silence and stealth were vital, and so was a good defense, because the unrecognized sound was alien and deafening. You didn't know what you might find. Quietly we made our way to the back porch to peek through windows to see what was happening. With shock, disbelief, and relief, we found two peacocks standing a few feet from the back door, hollering as loud as they possibly could, and looking in through the window of the back door. We figured they had seen the yard light and had flown toward it from out of the dark unknown.

They were extremely agitated and tense, probably even more terrified from their flight and where they found themselves than the rest of us had been terrified of them, before we knew what was making the noise. As soon as they saw us through the screen door, they really bellowed. You actually had to cover your ears because they ached from the sound.

The peacocks paced, flapped, and grew steadily more upset and even louder, although we didn't think they could have been louder. After several minutes that seemed like hours, they flew up into a walnut tree by the side of the house. It was an enormous old tree about eighty feet or more in height. There were three walnut trees of that size in the side yard, and maybe their height felt like a safe haven for the peacocks.

They stayed there all night. We saw them briefly in the morning, their brilliant, deep azure plumage gleaming in the morning sunlight. One flew out of the tree and down into the neighboring orchard, and the other followed a few moments later. It looked like they had been on their way somewhere, or on their way from somewhere, but for some reason they decided to stay close by.

Over the next few days they wandered peacefully about, keeping their distance from the flock although never too far away. They seemed to like the area and appeared to be relaxed in their new surroundings.

One evening, as we were quietly watching the chickens and the Guineas make their way through the chickenyard door, preparing to settle in for the night, one of the peacocks seemed upset as the Guineas slowly made their way into the chickenyard. He paced back and forth along the outer fence of the chickenyard but didn't go through the door. After all, he was many times the size of a Guinea or a chicken. The chickenyard must have appeared tiny to him, although it was spacious for the flock.

This scenario repeated itself for a few more days, and usually both peacocks behaved the same way. One peacock seemed to be more retiring than the other, but they both seemed to want to follow the Guinea hens. In fact, they seemed to be very interested in the Guinea hens. The male Guinea was not comfortable with this and seemed to want to rush at them one moment and to back away the next. His entire head wasn't much larger than the peacocks' bills. The Guinea hens appeared to pay the peacocks little or no attention, and the chickens were naturally completely unconcerned.

It was a difficult decision, but finally a very large, new flight pen was constructed along the west side of the entire shop-garage-shed complex. The pen was not the same as an open orchard, but it offered safety for the peacocks and also safety for the chickens, the Guinea hens, and especially the male Guinea. Meanwhile the peacocks seemed to feel more and more at home, and came closer and closer to following the Guineas into the chickenyard, every evening at dusk. The Guineas had begun to stay unusually close to the chickens, and given the current state of affairs, that seemed to be a wise decision on their part. They intermingled with the Rhode Island Reds, who didn't care at all about the peacocks. The flock simply lived on.

At last the peacocks' new home was completed, and it was time. One evening as the chickens and the Guineas were inside the chickenyard and began to disappear into the chickenhouse for the night, cracked corn was quietly spread just inside the open door of the chickenyard, and more was spread further into the depths of the chickenyard itself.

With great interest, the peacocks watched this happen. When no one was close by and the last of the chickens and Guineas were heading inside and out of sight, the peacocks ventured to the outermost kernels and began to eat. They were very hungry, wolfed down the cracked corn, and didn't hesitate for a moment but followed the trail of cracked corn into the chickenyard. Further and further into the depths of the chickenyard they went, eating as fast as they were able to peck at the cracked corn. It was upsetting to see, because it meant they must have been half starved all along.

Then the door to the chickenyard was closed, they were inside, and they actually didn't care. They continued to eat. After a while, when the cracked corn was nearly gone, we stepped softly into the chickenyard. One by one, we captured the peacocks, no small feat because peacocks are quite strong. They were not as quick on their feet as chickens were, and not nearly as fast as Guineas were. But if you didn't hold their bodies with their wings held in at their sides, you stood almost no chance of holding on to them, and a very good chance of being beaten about your head and arms with their large, strong wings.

You also had to maintain firm footing while holding them because they were heavy and struggled enough to offset your balance, and you both could easily have gone down while you were holding on for dear life.

One by one they were carried to their new home, not an easy task because they were so large. Once there, they had room to fly and room to run, and perhaps best of all, at least after they calmed down, they had a feeder and waterer of their own.

At first they were understandably nervous and didn't want anybody close to them, so they were left alone for a little while. A short time later, they began to eat again. Still hungry, they were grabbing mouthfuls of food. We were glad that they were in their new home at last, if for no other reason than to know that they had healthy food to eat and plenty of it, and to know that they were safe. The chickens and Guineas had gone to roost and were snoring away in a spread-out bundle that gently rose and fell.

In a small corner of a part of the peacocks' enclosure, one peacock and a molting hen wandered along the chicken-wire wall.

Eventually the time came when only one peacock remained. The other peacock was in a new home with his own peahen and lots of space. We felt the peacock that was left needed to find a suitable and permanent home where he could be free.

We took him to a sanctuary not far away, where he was welcomed. They said that peacocks are auspicious, nice to know but in a way not really a surprise. We had already felt graced by their presence in our lives as they were so beautiful and serene, and these had been well-behaved. The grounds there were peaceful and well kept, with flowering trees, shrubs, green lawns and green fields covering many acres. There were already several iridescent peacocks and peahens wandering safe and free.

The setting was extraordinary, and the experience sublime. This was a perfect way for the peacock to leave our home for a better one. He joined several white peahens in a wire-covered pen, where they remained only until they all felt at home enough to stay on the premises. Then they were allowed their freedom. As long as they had been with us, the peacocks were beautiful, regal creatures with amiable natures. Then they had moved on to better lives.

The chickens did not appear to miss the peacocks at all. The peacocks had merely been a shiny azure presence as far as the chickens were concerned, but after they were gone, the Guineas did not seem to feel the need to be surrounded by the flock, and actually began to stay in their own house most of the time. The arrival, sojourn and departure of the peacocks affected everyone except the implacable chickens, who as usual maintained their sense of equanimity throughout.

The Yellow-Golden Pheasant

Over time, other birds came to live on the property, often taking up residence not far from the chickens. The chickens always watched to see who arrived, who stayed on, and who left. But they always managed that agreeable and self-contained sense of well-being, cooing and chuckling gently to themselves, neither interacting with nor rejecting other residents.

Next door to the chickens, a pair of yellow-golden pheasants moved in and shared a chicken-wire fence with a peahen and the peacock, still in residence at the time. The hen had patterns of medium brown and cream, but the male pheasant was a brilliant yellow over nearly all of his body. The pair arrived with a pair of golden pheasants. This male was an intense red-orange color. The female that lived with him was also brown and patterned, although her colors were a bit darker and more intense than the other hen. The second pair lived around the corner from the chickens, didn't share a wall with anyone else, and were quiet and content.

However, the little yellow-golden pheasant was a completely different story. He was smaller than the golden pheasant, but he was an aggressive and confident soul. He was a beautiful bird with feathers the color of a very ripe lemon. He had soft, light-brown barring on his extremely long and elegant tail, and around his neck. His eyes were button bright with yellow tones in them, giving him the appearance of intently staring at you whenever you glanced at him.

He was cheerful and completely self-absorbed. He spent a great deal of time pacing and flying up and down in his house and yard area, but this wasn't nervous movement. It was more like prancing, and often he was puffed out so that he seemed to appear larger than life. He apparently felt that he, the bright yellow-golden pheasant, definitely impressed the female who lived with him and who not surprisingly seemed rather shy and retiring. She was around him all day.

The difference between the yellow-golden pheasant and the golden pheasant was extraordinary and unexpected. The golden pheasant had an altogether pleasant personality and was not especially overconfident. While the golden pheasant went about his day in an easy-going, quiet manner, the little bright yellow-golden pheasant stared balefully at anyone, feathered or otherwise, that came anywhere near his corner of the world,

It seemed that this interesting, small, bright yellow bird always put on a show for the female that lived with him, or at least it appeared that she was probably the reason for his ostentatious behavior. But the full range of his ambitions was not immediately obvious.

One day, when taking care of the peafowl, we noticed that the yellow-golden pheasant was stalking back and forth, back and forth, along the wire fence that separated the peacock and a peahen from the area he and the little female pheasant shared. This pacing occurred whenever the peahen absentmindedly wandered near the dividing fence. She wasn't watching the little yellow-golden pheasant. However he was clearly watching her. She was at least four times his size.

On and on, day after day, this small pheasant watched, paced, and puffed out his feathers. He saw the chickens too, but he didn't seem to be interested in them, and that was just as well. They were their usual complacent selves, not paying much attention to him, although they did appear to watch him out of sheer curiosity now and then. Occasionally, their necks and bills were stretched out in his direction. This was not something they did to be friendly. It was what they did when they were cornering a mouse. It was altogether best that he didn't stare at them while pacing back and forth near their fence line.

Meanwhile it seemed wise to reinforce the fence between the peafowl and the yellow-golden pheasants. A tarp was folded several times and wrapped along the bottom of the fence. The tarp reached well above the height of the yellow-golden pheasant, so he was no longer able to see the peahen unless he was on a roost several feet away. Covering the fence at his level had to be done, because he had become obsessed and had been seen bill to bill, through the fence, with the peacock that was beginning to take notice of this arrogant little intruder. The yellow-golden pheasant was even smaller than the Guineas. The peacock would have won hands down, and the battle would probably have been merciless but swift, judging by the way the peacock was stretching his neck and bill toward the little pheasant while staring at him intently.

The tarp worked, and the little pheasant seemed calmer. Fortunately, after this

126

interlude he didn't try to impress the chickens that were considerably larger than he was. While the chickens enjoyed life and were basically easygoing, they did not like to feel cornered, and these particular chickens would never have allowed themselves to be bullied by something much smaller than they were.

The small pheasant seemed to adjust and seemed to be content in his own domain, apparently no longer giving much thought to his neighbors. We felt a twinge of guilt about the little hen.

Sarge was in our thoughts. Sarge would have kept an eagle eye on that little pheasant, but the new rooster was still a very quiet rooster. At times like these his behavior was actually a little embarrassing. He was a part of the flock, but he was not really in control of it. There could never be another Sarge, and in truth any comparisons were unfair. However it did seem strange that the new rooster didn't immediately stare down the little, bright-yellow individual that appeared to challenge everyone and everything whenever opportunity knocked. Fortunately this small, self-proclaimed ruler survived for a long time, and very fortunately, without injury.

The Kingsnake

Although there were various snakes here and there around the orchard and once in a while near the garden, they were never intrusive and were never a problem. The chickens observed them with interest as they always had done, but not with consternation. If they were not dangerous, snakes were inconsequential to the main events of the day, like foraging and dusting. The snakes were primarily gopher snakes and garter snakes, and most were quite small, although a few were of medium size.

Rattlesnakes didn't seem to be around, although watching out for them was important because of the small runoff creek that ran along one side of the property. On one occasion there might have been a rattlesnake in the garden area close by, but it was gone before it could be clearly seen. Another time a snake skin surfaced when winter squash were gathered in for storage. It had been hidden under large squash leaves and vines and had mostly fallen apart, but it still had faint patterns that could have belonged to a rattlesnake. At the narrow end, it had a rough area that could have been the beginning of a button, but it was so deteriorated that we really couldn't tell what it was.

Squash vines would have made a nice summer refuge for a snake. They weren't disturbed because they were producing squash treasures, they were watered so the ground beneath them was moist and cool, and their leaves were large with fairly long stalks, creating a sort of elevated blanket. But they also had a rough and raspy texture. In any event some snake, and not a small snake at that, had shed its skin there.

Out and around gently cooing chickens, in the garden, in the orchard and in the grasses around fruit trees were the places where we expected snakes to be found, if they were there at all. So we were surprised one day to notice a quick movement in the living room. We peered into the living room from the kitchen counter where our lunch was. There, crawling with great difficulty across the living room carpet, was a tiny kingsnake. It was only the size of an elongated pencil and was obviously terrified at finding itself in a completely alien environment, with its freedom of movement practically nonexistent because of the soft carpet.

It had entered through the front door that was open on this warm, early summer day, and a screen door that was cracked open, leaving a space for our now very old, deaf and nearly blind Australian shepherd to pry his way in whenever he wanted. He was nearly always with us but was also safe outside on the lawn, in the fenced yard. He knew his way around very well, but that screen door had to be propped open just a little for a paw to pull it open.

The tiny kingsnake made its way to the hearth of river rock and concrete, where we encouraged it to crawl into a bucket so we could carry it outside. We figured that having a kingsnake around was good, except not inside the house, so we carried it through the orchard to the fairly roomy pump house. We released it nearby in orchard grass, near a plum tree, and close to the creek bed. It had nice, soft grass to enjoy, sun in open areas and shade from fruit trees and walnut trees. We figured it would be happy there and would have plenty of cover as well. We hoped that it would stay.

It did stay. It moved back to the house, although it didn't come inside this time. It claimed our property and the area around our house, including the front and side yards, the patio, and the entire back area with shop, garage, wood pile, shed, garden, chicken house, orchard, and fruit trees as its own. We didn't see it very often but when we did, it was generally on its way around its turf, probably hunting, but it also looked like it was on patrol.

The kingsnake found its way back from out in the orchard.

It appeared decisive.

Once in a great while it lay quietly on the cool

concrete walkway just outside the back door, startling anybody who came outside. Occasionally it relaxed in a grassy area a short distance from the walkway.

It usually made its way along the outer shop wall, behind a redwood tree and around the outer wall of a tiny greenhouse, stretching out in front of a small bed of sage. The sage draped over a few cinder blocks and bloomed profusely in the spring and early summer, with flowers that were vivid shades of purple. The little kingsnake made itself more or less invisible as it comfortably relaxed in this area.

When disturbed, when hunting or when moving along for some purpose known only to itself, it often headed from the tiny greenhouse toward the chickenhouse by traveling under the carport to the shed, and from there, to the area around the chickenyard. Once in a great while it headed in the opposite direction, making its way through

Flower beds needed to be protected from playful dogs. These fenced areas were perfect for the kingsnake, who made its way just about wherever it wanted to go.

the fence that surrounded the patio and the yard. From there it either hugged the outer wall of the house as it made its way along the side yard into the front yard, or it followed the outer edge of the patio and continued along the outer edges of the yards. It knew its turf.

There were a couple of things that interested it on the patio. The first was a small wading pool that belonged to the dogs, who splashed around in it, throwing water up in the air and batting the water around, especially during the heat of summer. This wading pool attracted insects, and insects attracted frogs. Frogs attracted the kingsnake.

The second was a group of several bird feeders that one of us enjoyed constructing. The feeders were kept filled mostly with black oil sunflower seeds. The patio was frequently swept because birds flapped about when feeding, spilled sunflower seeds onto the concrete below, and didn't find them all. Mice enjoyed the leftovers, and the kingsnake enjoyed the mice. Once in a while, rats began to enjoy the sunflower seeds, but excess seed and the rats were quickly brought under control. The old barn had taught us a serious lesson about rats.

Every spring, we wondered when the kingsnake would appear from its winter lair that we thought was either under the woodpile or within a stack of nearby hay bales. The kingsnake seemed to appear just as we were wondering where it was, often when we were standing on the concrete walk outside the back door. We would glance down and there it would be, stretched out at our feet.

We frequently saw it in the chickenhouse and chickenyard, probably looking for mice and definitely looking for prey within the warren of gopher runs there. You could see it moving through them, a bit of dark grey brown and cream ring-like patterns visible near the top of a gopher mound for a brief moment, and then disappearing into another run. Although you were startled when you saw a snake's movement in a gopher tunnel near your feet, and you weren't sure just what kind of snake it was, if you watched you could eventually make out the telltale kingsnake pattern, and when the tail passed by, you could see that it was pointed. These were good hunting grounds, the kingsnake didn't bother anyone, and everyone was happy to know that it was around. We knew that kingsnakes prey on rattlesnakes.

One day, a fairly large gopher snake was making its way along the outside of the chickenyard, probably hunting for mice, frogs or gophers. It only took a few moments for the kingsnake to make its way around the redwood tree, along the greenhouse wall, through the carport and toward the gopher snake. By then the kingsnake was of comparable size and the gopher snake either left at some point or became a meal, as the gopher snake was never seen again. After several years, a perfectly shed kingsnake skin was found toward the front of the house. When gently pulled into a fairly straight line, the skin was over four feet long. The last few years the kingsnake was seen, it was over five feet long. Whenever it stretched out in front of the cinder blocks by the tiny greenhouse, you could count blocks visible behind it, measure them and arrive at a minimal length for the kingsnake. It was actually longer because it wasn't stretched out in a completely straight line.

The kingsnake wasn't handled, so an accurate measurement wasn't possible. It was already more accustomed to all of us than we would have liked. It didn't try to escape us, the dogs, the cats that had joined the household, or the horse, and it didn't pay any more attention to the chickens than they paid to it, which was none at all. It was safer if it was wary. It was a strikingly beautiful, seemingly good-natured, and healthy kingsnake.

One year, much of the neighboring pear orchard was removed, and the land was allowed to lie fallow for a few years. Tall weeds grew there, undergrowth was thick, and habitat was inviting for tiny animal life, amphibians, insects, birds of all kinds, rodents, raptors, foxes, coyotes, bobcats, and even mountain lions, and was obviously inviting for the kingsnake, too. For some reason, probably because they weren't fools, the chickens wandered only to the edges of this field, but no further.

The spring after the pear trees were removed, the kingsnake awoke and was seen in its usual territory. Then it was simply gone for a very long time. It was seen much later in the year, in the grassy area near the tiny greenhouse. After that it was not seen again. There was a sense from suspicious markings in soil here and there that it came to overwinter in its old haunts and then moved out into good hunting grounds in the fallow field, or at least went back and forth for a while. After a while it was simply gone, or at least we didn't see it and didn't find any evidence that it was around.

There was really no reason to assume bad things. Right next door, a veritable banquet of opportunity had opened up for it. Still, we'd have liked to see it now and then, as it had become a more or less invisible part of the household. It had cleaned up the chickens' area for many years, although it couldn't possibly have consumed all the mice and gophers there. Once in a while you saw trembling mice very quietly and tentatively crouched on top of the ground, and you knew that the kingsnake was nearby, probably under your feet in a burrow. Naturally we missed it.

The more you grew attached to various life forms around you, the more you realized how much you didn't know or understand. Your senses told you that there was a huge world of knowledge and different ways of being that you didn't appreciate, because you didn't recognize the details or the vastness of it all. You knew the chickens lived in a very complex world of their own, and now a kingsnake had lived within a circle of trust for many years. This might seem strange, but to us, this was an extraordinary gift.

Chapter 9

Long Live the Chickens

The Flock Dwindles
Deprivation
There Will Always Be Chickens

When you lived for many years alongside chickens, observed them, respected them and were very fond of them, and then you faced change, that change was difficult for the heart to accept. Chickens were special. They were unique entities that made life richer and more fulfilling. Their eggs graced our table in many variations, however they themselves did not. They were our friends. But not everyone was their friend. They definitely had their share of predators and enemies. Within their own circle and as long as they were safe, they seemed to exhibit equanimity toward everything, more than many residents of Planet Earth seem able to do. There is really no description for a chicken except, well, chicken.

The Flock Dwindles

Over time, chickens were lost to infirmities and to old age. Fortunately there were no major outbreaks of some hideous, inscrutable, and indefinable disease, at least not that we knew. This was good news, because chickens, pheasants, and peacocks remained basically healthy. Chickens grew older, knobbier legs moved more slowly, and eggs were laid less often. There were slight losses of color in combs and wattles, and slightly less shiny or well-preened feathers. It was just aging.

In addition to younger chickens' occasionally replacing older chickens that passed away, there was one major rotation among the Rhode Island Reds. The flock that had been housed by our neighbors, and that then had occupied the sturdy chickenhouse, grew quite ancient and began to diminish in numbers, as chickens passed peacefully on to that Great Coop in the Sky.

Before they were completely gone, a new batch of young hens arrived and began to blend in with the older, more experienced hens. The ancient, ceremonial pecking order was in constant use and the older hens held their places. When it was their time, they did not pass on after having fallen from a coveted position within the flock. We were grateful for that. The rooster at hand also kept law and order and we always respected him, although there was of course never another Sarge.

As the years passed, most of the other birds also passed on of old age. The peacocks were the only additions that found wonderful new homes. All others were treated gently for any problems, including clipping overgrown toenails, administering vitamins, administering antiseptics to little scratches, or providing a soft and comfortable place in the sun where older legs and wings could stretch out and be warmed by sunshine. Eventually when it was their time, they passed away and were buried in soft grass under a fruit tree.

The younger hens were laying eggs and were content. There didn't seem to be disturbances or uprisings in the new chickenhouse, and thankfully Son of Sarge, or anything remotely like him, was long gone. It was hard to imagine that there could ever be more than one Son of Sarge in anyone's lifetime anyway.

As the flock diminished in size, it seemed kinder not to bring in a large number of young pullets or a young rooster. Chickens were not the only individuals passing on, and changes meant that a smaller flock seemed best.

One day, when there were only three ancient Rhode Island Red hens living in the chickenhouse and chickenyard, a friend came by with four tiny chickens that needed a home. There were three miniscule hens and one only slightly larger rooster, larger only because he seemed to have more tail feathers. These little chickens were Mille Fleurs, delicate brown, black and white chickens with a speckled pattern over their entire bodies.

They had fluffy feathers under their chins and looked a little as though they might be wearing thick, woolly scarves. They also had fairly long feathers that grew out from the sides of their feet, that were incidentally just as large and ungainly relative to their diminutive size as the huge, clawed, tripod feet were to the larger Rhode Island Reds. When the little Mille Fleurs walked, they moved in a sprightly and determined manner, those feathers at foot level not hindering them at all.

They had small, thick combs and wattles, and very bright eyes. They were not especially tame and once released into the chickenyard, were difficult to catch again. For such tiny chickens, they moved fast. Fortunately it wasn't necessary to catch them often, only if one seemed to need a close examination if he or she seemed out of sorts, or if toenails or spurs needed to be clipped because they'd grown too long for the little chickens' own comfort and safety.

These tiny chickens were about half the size of the Rhode Island Red hens. The larger hens were friendly enough, but the smaller group kept to itself and did not try to intermingle with them. There was more than enough room in the chickenyard and chickenhouse for the little chickens and the Reds to be together without any problems, since originally the space had been planned for a flock of Rhode Island Red chickens.

The little chickens did not go outside the chickenyard, although we wished they could have experienced freedom in the great outdoors. They were too tiny and would have made a nice meal for a hawk. Predators could have easily carried them away. Although the little chickens were quick, feisty and flew very well when they thought there was need, there was little doubt that a skunk or a raccoon could have caught one or two, or four. Most of the time the little ones quietly scratched and ate, clucked and visited with each other, and were altogether pleasant and sweet-natured, if not as innately calm as the Silkies had been.

Since the three Rhode Island Red hens were so elderly and therefore vulnerable, they remained in the chickenyard too. The two groups scratched in the hay that was spread out for them now and then. It had seeds that sprouted into grasses and oats, creating space for fat insects and earthworms. A small container was filled with greens from the garden plus occasional ripe fruit, and as usual, extra ripe apricots fell down into their chickenyard. Everybody seemed happy, and basically everybody was compatible. The little chickens did not have aggressive natures, and neither did the three Rhode Island Reds. A marvelous peace reigned in the chickenyard and in the chickenhouse.

Interestingly, the little Mille Fleur rooster seemed to take on the duties of watching over all of the hens, both small and large. He was an amiable rooster

whose high pitched crowing was heard from morning until dusk every day. Like the small hens he was not aggressive, possessing instead a common sense attitude that showed itself when he alerted all the hens, regardless of size, to food, or to the shadow of a hawk, or to anything else he figured was important. There was no impatience and no domineering attitude. He performed his duties in a friendly, efficient, and business-like manner.

While he always included the whole chickenyard when he had something to communicate, he stayed around the group of little hens. He was so tiny, it would have been next to impossible to notice rooster body language had not Sarge already educated us along those lines. After all the little rooster was still a rooster, with rippling, cascading tail feathers and striking comb and wattles, large enough for his diminutive size but still small. He had deep, glistening chestnut colors over his entire body but especially concentrated in a few places on his back and his wings. The speckling pattern was attractive, uniform, and covered his whole self, even the feathers on his feet. He was a congenial, sprightly soul.

The elderly Rhode Island Reds weren't laying eggs any more and were simply enjoying the rest of their lives free of responsibility. When the little chickens began leaving eggs in the nest boxes, they were leaving real treats. These obviously weren't large eggs but were about two-thirds of the size of a medium-sized Rhode Island Red egg, still very large eggs when you considered the size of the hens laying them.

The Mille Fleur eggs were light brown and a bit more elongated than Rhode Island Red eggs were, but otherwise they were exactly the same as any other fresh eggs, with firm whites and yellow-orange yolks that didn't break easily. There is nothing quite like a fresh egg laid by a chicken that is allowed to scratch, has a varied diet, and is healthy because she's living in a healthy environment. A pleasant and peaceful existence somehow comes across in the food produced and that you collect and eat.

Like the larger hens, these little chickens observed firm, structured social rules within their own small, complex, chicken society, even though there were so few of them. They were a fascinating little group. They gobbled up bugs and worms, scratched for food, scratched out comfortable depressions for lounging, hovered en masse around The Nest Box, and enjoyed a tranquil life.

They also ran toward food when the little rooster called them because he had discovered something burrowing into the soft soil under hay in the chickenyard, or had found something scurrying away from his watchful eyes.

They were a treat to watch when they ran. This was something you didn't expect, and it felt a little inconsistent with their otherwise matter-of-fact approach to life. There was the usual rolling from side to side because of the generic chicken pear shape, even though they were leaner than Rhode Island Reds, but the rolling seemed to be accented because of the fairly long feathers on their feet. They had to lift their feet completely off the ground and slap them back down while they were running. The feathers appeared almost like snowshoes, only from each foot they stretched out from side to side rather than front to back. How those foot feathers stayed intact and nice-looking was a complete mystery. How those foot feathers had evolved in the first place was a mystery, because you didn't think that survival of the species was enhanced by snowshoe foot feathers.

Scratching didn't create large holes, but instead resulted in petite depressions in the soil. The same food was consumed, just less of it. Only one nest box was used for a roosting area at night, because all the little chickens were able to fit into one nest box. They settled into deep shavings or perched on the sides, arranging themselves very comfortably there. They looked through the fence they had in common with the pheasant, peering at him just as the Rhode Island Reds did, but only once in a while, just as the Rhode Island Reds did. The only difference was that they were nearly at eye level with him. Theirs was the normal, self-contained world of all chickens.

When you were trying to catch them, you were taken by surprise at how quickly they ran and also flew across the chickenyard. Even though they were tiny, they moved full speed ahead. They also seemed to possess a measure of wisdom and common sense, and unlike Silkies who were so sweet-natured, they were rather grounded and determined in their demeanor. They respected other types of life, but on the whole and like every other chicken before them, other life was not of much consequence to their own existence, as long as they themselves remained safe and were able to continue finding food.

These tiny chickens reinforced the glimmer of a suspicion that all things considered, chicken culture was maybe not easy to understand, not when you looked closely at it. Also, these little ones had their chicken ways, but those ways were neither as pronounced nor as easily seen as the Rhode Island Reds' detailed routines. This was probably because the Mille Fleurs were so small, their

The little Mille Fleurs were alert. You couldn't photograph them easily because they were always one step ahead of you.

body language wasn't always easy to see except by another chicken. And they were not as docile as the Silkies had been. However, they were chickens, and therefore they demonstrated the timeless ways of all chickens. It almost seemed we were not mindful of the possibility of the existence of substrata within chicken culture. Meanwhile the tiny Mille Fleurs flourished and maintained that universal chicken composure.

Deprivation

There were several major changes that happened over a period of several years. They involved loss, and generally they were the natural events that happen in everyone's life. The flock had dwindled due to old age. The chicken population consisted only of Mille Fleurs, since the extremely elderly Rhode Island Red hens had passed away from natural causes.

Actually Mille Fleur numbers grew slightly when one fall, a tiny Mille Fleur decided to set on four eggs. They all hatched, and she happily raised them, keeping a sharp eye on anyone or anything that came remotely close to her little family.

At first, mother and chicks were confined to a nest box with raised sides, enough to prevent the tiny babies from escaping, but not so high that the mother hen would be unable to leave for a few moments now and then to stretch, eat, and drink. A small feeder and waterer were secured to the sides of the nest box, low enough so the babies could reach them but just above the fresh pine shavings that kept their little home clean and warm. The placement was critical because the chicks were so small, they could hardly walk across pine shavings, but they had to be able to eat and drink whenever they wanted.

Little chicks grow quickly and soon scurry here and there, investigating their surroundings. After a very short time, another home was fashioned in a pet carrier and situated just barely above the floor of the chickenhouse. It also was filled with fresh pine shavings, and its door was left permanently open with a ramp of shavings leading up to the door and inside, so hen and chicks could enter and leave at will.

The feeder and waterer were placed on a very low platform near their new home. The babies needed food specially made for growing chicks, and it had to be kept close by but situated in such a way that shavings didn't spill into the feeder or the waterer, and yet tiny chicks could still reach what they needed. That was tricky but vital, and these were very tiny chicks. The baby Mille Fleurs ran all over their little house, around and over each other and in circles around their mother, but never far away from her.

The tiny mother hen took excellent care of her chicks, and they blossomed. She was completely attentive to them, and that was critical because the weather was turning colder. Usually hens set in spring or early summer, but for some reason this little chicken had entertained different ideas that year. She had hatched these chicks about four months later than usual, past summer months when there was time

When she was setting, she didn't leave her nest. She was a small, speckled, feathered comforter.

for them to grow adult feathers and fill out for colder weather ahead. These fortunate chicks had a mother that kept them toasty warm with her fluffed out feathers. She prodded them to eat and drink, frequently leading them to the feeder and waterer.

Time passed too quickly and suddenly there they were, mother and babies, scratching in the hay and moist soil of the chickenyard. The chicks were truly tiny bundles of fluff that closely followed their mother's every move around the chickenyard and cuddled under her wings for naps. The main waterer had been switched to one that had a narrow, shallow reservoir, so chicks wouldn't accidentally fall in and be unable to climb out. Like all chicks, these tiny babies were curious, full of energy, and they were really very fast. They seemed to enjoy checking out anything and everything, running round and round each other and sprinting back and forth all over the chickenyard. They jumped and ran, twirled, took off flapping their tiny developing wings, and enjoyed being alive.

The mother hen seemed alarmed at times because her babies literally ran circles around her most of the day. She wanted to know where each one was at every moment and more or less constantly clucked that even, rhythmic cluck that mother hens use to gather their chicks. When they were still quite small, the chicks came running, but as they grew larger they were more independent and drove their mother to distraction, even though they were never very far from her.

When the little group first ventured into the chickenyard, the mother hen remained puffed out and every few moments plopped down and spread her wings slightly, inviting the chicks to hurry under her feathers and stay warm and safe. The weather was chilly by then. As the chicks grew and were able to retain body heat for longer increments of time away from her, she scratched and foraged about the chickenyard for a few moments longer before settling herself again, so the chicks could warm themselves under her feathers.

When she was scratching and pecking at some tidbit, her chicks mimicked her and learned by example how to forage in those time-honored chicken ways. They still played and ran, but they never ventured far from her, and there was no worry that they would try to find an opening into the great outdoors beyond the chickenyard. The little family was like a small, energetic solar system with the hen at its center.

Eventually the tiny Mille Fleurs began to lose their downy feathers and to grow their adult plumage. They were still basically all the same size, and they still followed their mother around, trying to crowd under her wings when they could, although they were about half grown by now and her little wings couldn't reach over all of them at one time. She clucked to them less and less, and finally she began to wander on her own and to eat in earnest, next to the other hens and the delicate little rooster.

All this time he had watched the entire process of the chicks' hatching and growing with great interest but had remained close to the other hens, basically leaving the diminutive mother and her chicks alone. Had they been in danger, we figured that he would have intervened as any responsible rooster would have done, but we never saw it happen.

Time passed, and the young chickens grew into full adult plumage and began to differ a little, one from another. It turned out that there were three young roosters and one young hen. Since the chickenhouse and chickenyard were peaceful territory, only one rooster could remain. The original rooster stayed and the three young roosters, with their whole lives ahead of them, found new homes.

The young hen stayed. By remaining close to her mother, she found herself integrated into the group of adults at least until she began to lay eggs of her own. Then her mother no longer protected her as much, and she seemed to be just slightly distant from the others. She was on the bottom rung of the pecking order, although her mother was often close by and didn't seem to participate in pecking order procedure, at least not much, either for herself or for her daughter. The other hens followed the rules. It was painful to see the baby being sort of shoved this way and that way by the others, but it was the natural way of chickens, and it was the law. There wasn't anything that could or should have been done about it. She was all right, never hurt, although very surprised at first and a little nervous for a while, but she adapted.

Her mother still protected her just a little. When her mother found a particularly juicy morsel to eat, she would call her now-adult daughter and allow her to eat it, even though mother and daughter were the same size. The mother hen continued this behavior for years. We didn't know if this was a normal pattern for Mille Fleurs, but we thought the gestures were gracious and generous.

There Will Always Be Chickens

Although the flock was small now, it carried on, as chickens will always carry on. It survived, following the timeless traditions of all flocks. The behavior and chicken culture it exhibited were no different than that taught to us by Sarge and his hens, who had entered our lives so many years before. The flock was quieter, the chickens were smaller, and there were fewer of them, but the ways of chickendom continued on, sunrise to sunset, season after season, year after year, because chicken cycles are ageless and time-honored.

There was a comfortable security when you knew that the way in which chickens had allowed you to coexist alongside them in years past was the same way in which the current chickens accepted your existence. You were acknowledged especially when you brought food, but that was about it. As before, you lived next to them and you enjoyed them, but you were not a part of their daily plans. Their habits were reliable that way.

It's true that their home, yard and food were provided for them, but the universal assumption, their universal assumption, was that these things were always provided for them. It was normal. It was supposed to be that way, and it didn't mean that they owed anybody anything, or that they were subservient to anyone. That wasn't the way they did things. The concept of debt or payback was irrelevant, because this was the way of the natural world at work, and we were a part of their natural environment.

There is a truth for everything, ecological integration is normal, and our integration into their world included providing for them, since the emphasis was on their world, not ours. Whether proto-chickens lived in the jungle or whether they had scales rather than feathers at one time, they took their rightful place in the universe, although they probably wouldn't have been the softly chuckling, clucking, and cooing feathered friends that lived close to our hearts.

Chickens will go on. They will not be broken. They will continue to please themselves in their own daily routines, and to endear themselves to many who have been introduced to their charms. They will also scratch about in the dirt, decimate your garden, and will no doubt continue to be the subjects of a multitude of recipes from around the world.

They are Chicken, and that is more than enough for them to cast their spell of fascination and enchantment upon whoever chooses to invite them into his or her life. They visit quietly with each other as they forage. They surge into places that they can destroy, like a feathered tide obliterating row after row of young, tender lettuce. It is exasperating when chickens, soft soil, and vegetable gardens are placed at odds that cannot be resolved with any reasoning from human to chicken. Simultaneously, their soft, contented voices, when they are happily resting or pecking at grasses or insects, are a soothing balm in an otherwise busy and often harsh world. They are unique, strange, and precious creatures, and the world would be impoverished without them.

Some current residents.

Epilogue

The whole original chicken experience was so full of color for the senses that it was a living kaleidoscope. It was as awe-inspiring as a clear night sky full of stars and northern lights. It also covered the entire range of possible emotions, at all levels. That continues on.

For these reasons and more it is quite impossible to figure that these amazingly complex, feathered bundles do not have minds, hearts and souls. Even though empirical science cannot prove that, and theoretical science would be obliged to dismiss it, there comes a point when you realize that chickens are not necessarily what many have assumed chickens to be, that is, providers of eggs and drumsticks and not much more.

There comes a point at which you have to look at a chicken and wonder what other incorrect assumptions you've assimilated in your lifetime, and how far down you need to dig to turn over beliefs that have become stale and unappetizing, and maybe false. It isn't so much a matter of shrugging away some of those things you have always known as much as it is opening the eyes of your mind to what gifts have been given you. It's about the importance of what is around you.

This is not to say that a chicken can eat every shred of lettuce you've ever planted, and can peck a hole, just one hole, in every nearly ripened tomato as you've patiently watched them all develop, and there can be no complaining. It is a chicken's nature to forage, but there is nothing quite the same as fresh lettuce and sun-ripened tomatoes in a salad. Conflict exists.

If you plant beautiful primroses and feel peace and beauty overcome you while you're contemplating a particularly large and velveteen primrose, you will be startled if a giant yellow, scaled leg with a huge, flexible, tripod foot with claws suddenly enters your field of vision and rakes over the lovely blossom, leaving it shredded and strewn over the moist earth. There are dichotomies.

There is always juxtaposition somewhere. The grace of every interaction is the dance performed by the positives and negatives on either side of the fulcrum, and this includes any knowledge that is gained and further enriched because the soul has grown. Perhaps normalcy is nothing more than the wavering, often fragile equilibrium hovering between two truths, a delicate primrose and soft clucking sounds nearby, tender lettuce leaves and a large tripod foot, or even Sarge and Son of Sarge.

Meanwhile, experiencing life's high points and low points can be exhausting, even though that's how life is. Perhaps that is why living alongside chickens, seeing how complex they really are, and observing how they look after each other as they maintain the integrity of the flock is humbling. The chickens that accepted us into their lives had individual personalities, but the only chicken that wasn't amiable was Son of Sarge who was definitely an anomaly. Sarge was treasured even more when we saw him beside Son of Sarge. A lot more.

Probably one of the most precious perceptions is seeing how generous chickens are, quite simply by living. They remain happy and content with no animosity toward anybody or anything, as long as they are just allowed to exist. They don't appear to harbor anger or grudges, and their moods seem to swing back into a contented, harmonious existence not long after they've been disturbed for some reason, as long as they are safe.

This is easy to understand if the assumption is that chickens are not intelligent enough to know better, but when they allow you to live near them and wander in their midst for years, the thought that they are not intelligent in their own way doesn't wash. It doesn't take imagination to see how chickens live their lives. All you have to do is watch them.

Not everyone likes chickens, just as not everyone enjoys the same activities, the same foods, the same books, the same videos or the same people. What a boring place the world would be if everybody liked the same things. There are those who will take issue with what is written here, but I suppose I'd say that it's easy to be humbled by chickens, for instance when you attempt to chase them out of your garden. It's amazing how quickly they can perform an about face and whisk past you, landing right back in that delectable row of snow peas they were enjoying before you arrived.

Perhaps one of the many lessons to learn from chickens and their life style is to respect what you thought wouldn't demand respect from you. Respect, even for chickens. Respect definitely for chickens.

Long live the flock!

Index

The author was raised in northern California, has degrees in anthropology and wildlife biology, graduate work in ethnomusicology, and is an artist (www.rootlets.com).

She currently lives in northern California, there is a walnut orchard out back, and there are chickens. They are a source of wonder, amazement, and sometimes exasperation too, but they always remain serenely true to their nature and are therefore a source of tranquil reliability, forever close to one's heart.

The soul walks not upon a line,
neither does it grow like a reed.
The soul unfolds itself,
like a lotus of countless petals.

Kahlil Gibran

www.ingramcontent.com/pod-product-compliance
Lightning Source LLC
Chambersburg PA
CBHW041542260326
41914CB00015B/1519

* 9 7 8 0 9 8 5 5 1 0 9 7 8 *